THE MAGIC CARPET
AND OTHER TALES

The Magic Carpet

and Other Tales

RETOLD BY *Ellen Douglas*
WITH THE ILLUSTRATIONS OF
Walter Anderson

University Press of Mississippi
JACKSON AND LONDON

Text copyright © 1987 by Ellen Douglas
All rights reserved

Illustrations copyright © 1987
by the Walter I. Anderson Estate
All rights reserved

Printed in Japan

91 90 89 88 87   5 4 3 2 1

*Library of Congress Catalog
Card Number: 87-10434
Library of Congress Cataloging in
Publication Data on page 186
British Cataloguing in Publication
data available*

The illustrations in this book are reproduced from linoleum
block prints designed by Walter I. Anderson and hand-
painted by Adele Anderson Lawton. Carolyn Anderson
pulled the prints from the original blocks.

Designed by John Langston and JoAnne Prichard
ISBN 0-87805-327-1

To the grandchildren of Walter Anderson

Mark, Amelia, Jason, Chris, Rosalie, Mary, Dodie, Moira, Vanja, and Josh

and to my grandchildren

Ayres, Brooks, Corinne, Taylor, and Isaac

CONTENTS

ACKNOWLEDGMENTS

Walter Anderson's widow Agnes, his daughter Mary Pickard, and his niece Adele Lawton were a source of inspiration, advice, and support to me and to the publisher in the planning and making of this book.

I would also like to thank the staffs of the Millsaps College Library and the Eudora Welty Library in Jackson, Mississippi, and of the de Grummond Children's Literature Collection in the McCain Library at the University of Southern Mississippi for their patience and generous assistance.

INTRODUCTION

Stepping into the world of fairy tales—a world I have moved into and out of during sixty years and more, but scarcely ever *thought* about—beginning to read versions of stories and to think about how to retell them, I was struck with their chameleon capacity to change color, even to drop a leg or a tail, so to speak, in order to avoid capture; to vanish and then, somewhere far off, to grow another and reappear.

Every fairy story I know, now I think of it, has in my memory and imagination a changing life. I hear my mother's voice or the voice of an aunt or a grandmother reading and telling again and again her own favorites. I see myself lying in bed in the early morning between my aunt and uncle in a big room made secret and inaccessible by the enclosed stair one must climb to reach it. I am listening. Or I am sitting on a stool beside my grandmother's brown wicker rocker, or lying in my own bed in a curious white sheet tent with a croup kettle hissing and the voice of my invisible mother, reading, reading, reading, until I fall asleep to the music of the tale. Then again, I hear my own voice, reading to my children and my grand-children—or just telling: leaving out, adding, emphasizing, forgetting, making the stories over to suit them and me.

So they are chameleon, these tales, adapting to the color of every voice, pulsing now green and now brown against leaf or bark, blowing up the scarlet bubbles in their tiny throats, slithering away, vanishing and returning.

But then, in another sense, they seem to have sunk into my memory and become, as it were, types of themselves, a part of the very structure of my imagination. In the same way, when I hear the word *tree*—not oak or elm or pecan—a rooted, branching, leafy image springs to mind. But it is an image that changes when I hear, "I mean dogwood tree." Or pine tree in the snow, or maple tree in October, or tulip magnolia already blooming in February.

I know King Arthur as the type of the perfect king, but I know him, too, from *The Boys' King Arthur* with the Wyeth illustrations. I even see Wyeth's king, narrow-eyed and blonde-bearded, sad and slightly wicked-looking (although of course he is not wicked). And I see Lancelot, wild and ragged, lying on a rock in the wilderness, in the shadow of a sinister forest. He is "wood," the story tells me (Malory, edited by Sidney Lanier), and the glamour and mystery of that old word for crazy is added to the picture.

It is this double sense of changing specificity and unchanging type that gives me the courage to retell these tales—the knowledge that they are retold in every generation in as many voices as there are writers and tellers who care for them. Never mind that there are echoes from the past in my voice—how could it be otherwise? Never mind that I am trailing along behind giants like Andersen and the Brothers Grimm and Perrault, behind Basile's robust *Pentamarone* and the sophisticated court tales of Madame de Beaumont and

Madame D'Aulnoy—not to mention Jacob's *English Fairy Tales* and the Appalachian Jack tales and Aesop and Apuleius and the *Gesta Romanorum*—and even Euripedes. And not to mention, either, the distinguished translators and re-creators in English, from Malory's *Morte D'Arthur* and Adlington's Apuleius and Payne and Burton's *Thousand Nights and a Night* to Gilbert Murray's Euripides and Horace Gregory's Ovid and Randall Jarrell's Grimm.

All these voices and others I have heard and they have sunk deep into my imagination. They tell me that I can never make fairy tales or myths my own. They belong to the world, to tellers and listeners everywhere, always the same and always different.

When I first saw the beautiful Walter Anderson illustrations for these tales (and, of course, the tales were selected for this book *because* Anderson had illustrated them), I was sure that he was saying with his pictures the same thing I had been saying to myself about *telling*. For there is a double quality to the illustrations: they are as hieratic, as mythic as images from an Egyptian tomb or a medieval church, and as quirky and individual as a known voice. And I think it would have pleased him—as it does me—that his niece Adele Anderson Lawton, in a new generation of makers, has joined her vision to his to give the illustrations their jewel-like colors.

Walter Inglis Anderson (1903–1965), whose watercolors, drawings, block prints, murals, and pottery have in the years since his death been more and more widely recognized for their beauty and originality, made the linoleum blocks, reproductions of which illustrate this book, at a time (between 1945 and 1948) when he was living with his wife and four children in Gautier, Mississippi. The fairy tale illustrations and the other works of the period (illustrations for *The Odyssey* and *The Iliad, Paradise Lost, Don Quixote,* and

Alice in Wonderland, an ABC book, nursery rhymes, and an overwhelming flood of sketches and water-colors of the world around him) were born of a complex personal, political, and artistic intent: the desire to entertain his own children, the conviction that good art should be made available to people at prices they could pay (the original prints were sold for one dollar per foot), and the burning, obsessive, dedicated discipline of the committed artist.

The "overmantels," as he called the fairy tale pictures, were cut from battleship linoleum purchased at the local army-surplus store and printed on the reverse side of faded wallpaper scrounged from a paint and wallpaper store—the dimensions of the wallpaper governing the final shape and price of the prints. (Thus a print six feet long by eighteen inches wide—the size of most of the original prints reproduced in this book—sold for six dollars.)

In the same sense, one might say that the cave paintings at Lescaux which he so admired were to a degree influenced by the accidents of the surface on which they were painted. But Walter Anderson, of course, was no primitive. He was a deeply thoughtful, highly sophisticated artist, a prize-winning student and graduate of the Pennsylvania Academy of the Fine Arts, who, as a young man, served his time wandering and studying in the museums of Europe. His gift to us is one of powerful and compelling images, always his own, but grounded in his knowledge of the world's art.

Do you remember as a child turning the pages of a new book to see how many pictures there were and whether you liked them—the disappointment you felt in one of those worthless books that had only black and white pictures—or, worse, no pictures at all, not even a frontispiece? Of course you never noticed the *name* of the illustrator—or for that matter, the name of the teller. (I suppose as a child I must have thought

Grimm and Andersen wrote in a universally under-stood language.) But the pictures! Like Wyeth's Arthur, there are certain pictures stamped for me from childhood on certain stories: Heath Robinson's evil-clawed man-beast (How could anyone, even a maiden so saintly as Beauty, possibly consent to marry him?); Psyche clutching a diaphanous white nightgown to her bosom and gazing down, lamp in hand, at a sleeping Cupid (Where did I see that pic-ture? I seem to remember it not in a book, but on a wall in my grandmother's house); Dore's Puss, the dead mouse hanging at his belt, the hat like D'Artag-non's and the boots that look as if they were finished off with pinking shears. Now, for my grandchildren and their children, Walter Anderson will be in this company—Thumbelina floating seaward among crabs and leaping fish and red-winged blackbirds; Psyche standing breast to breast with Cupid, her torch raised high; the cat princess, pouncing, even on her wedding night, on one last hapless mouse.

One word about the explicators of fairy tales—the literature of explanation—psychological, anthropo-logical, religious, political. There must surely be more explications of fairy tales than there are of Hamlet, and these, too, change with every generation. The Freudians say this and the Jungians say that. Frazer speaks, and Lang and Bettelheim. And then there are the Marxists and the feminists. The teller of tales may read all these with interest, even with fascination, but she must finally forget (forgetting is as much a part of telling as remembering) the interpreters and put her attention on the tale.

And then? And then? What happened next, Grand-mother? are the questions the listener asks, and so the teller seeks the deeds, the language, the images that will keep the listener under the spell of the tale.

Once more the sleeping maiden wakes. Once more the ogre is outwitted, the dragon slain. Goat and donkey, fisherman and sailor, prince and princess, god and mortal maiden triumph once more by wit and strength and beauty and magic over the forces of evil that haunt all our dreams.

Ellen Douglas

THE MAGIC CARPET
AND OTHER TALES

The Magic Carpet

All lovers of fairy tales know how in the days of yore and time long gone before, there was a sultan in Baghdad who, because his wife betrayed him, vowed vengeance against all the women in the world. Thereafter he had brought to his chamber every night a young virgin whom he deflowered (everything here is put in the most circumspect terms) and in the morning, having had his pleasure of her, sent her to be—there is no other word for it—strangled. And that the daughter of his vizier, Shahrazad (whose name is sometimes spelled one way and sometimes another), resolving to save her sisters from such a fate, went to her father and said, "How long must this slaughter endure, my father? Let me, I pray you, go to the sultan tonight. Perhaps I can so charm him that I will break this dreadful cycle." Her father, horrified, did all he could to dissuade her. But Shahrazad persisted, saying that she had a plan in mind and that if her plan failed she would go to her death glorious, while if it succeeded she would have done a service to all women everywhere.

And so at last her father consented.

3

When she went in to the sultan that night, Shahrazad, as she had agreed beforehand with her sister Dunyazad, asked as a boon if Dunyazad might spend the night at the foot of the sultan's couch and be near her to bid her a last farewell in the morning. To this the sultan consented.

Of course, as we all know, Dunyazad, before daybreak asked Shahrazad to while away the dark hour with a story, and thus began the thousand nights and a night on every one of which the sultan had his will of Shahrazad and she, to put off her death, told a story so fascinating that the sultan, when she broke off at dawn, could not bear to have her killed before he heard the end of it and so kept her alive until the following night.

At length, after the thousandth night, so the story goes, charmed by Shahrazad's wit and beauty, the sultan made her his bride. Such were happy endings in those days.

The story of Prince Ahmad and the fairy Peri Banu,

which is sometimes called "The Magic Carpet," is one of these tales—or rather, altogether, it is a number of them, half a dozen of so, and occupied several nights in the marathon of Shahrazad's tale-telling.

Know that long ago there was a sultan of India who had three sons, the princes Husayn, Ali, and Ahmad. He had also a niece and ward, Princess Nur al-Ninar, the daughter of his younger brother, who, dying early, left his only child as ward to his brother. This young girl, who, as she grew up, excelled all the maidens in the land in wit and beauty, spent her childhood in play and comradeship with her three cousins and, as she came to womanhood, all fell in love with her.

The king, knowing what havoc among the brothers

this rivalry might bring, called them before him. "I see, my sons," he said, "how dearly you love your cousin and how you vie for her affection. Rather than see you fall to quarreling out of love for her, I propose a contest. Let the three of you set out and travel through the world and bring back to me the most marvelous thing you see on your travels. He who brings the rarest of curiosities shall be husband to Princess Nur al-Ninar."

So the three, being obedient sons, agreed to this proposal and set out together. Three days they traveled until they came to a place where three roads met. Here they spent the night at an inn and the next day, vowing to meet here in a year's time, they disguised themselves as wandering merchants, and parted, each taking a separate road. So they wandered far and wide and in the course of the year had various adventures.

When the year was up, each returned, bearing what he was sure was the most wondrous thing in the world. The eldest, Husayn, brought with him—or rather was transported upon—a carpet, ordinary-looking enough, which in the twinkling of any eye would transport its owner to whatever place he wished to visit. The second, Ali, in his wanderings had come upon and purchased a spy glass, a little tube with glass in either end through which the owner could look and see whatever in the world he desired to see. The third, Prince Ahmad, brought a magical apple, the virtue of which was that whoever inhaled its fragrance would instantly be healed of his sickness, no matter how near death he might be.

Now when the brothers had met at the appointed place at the year's end and had shown each other their prizes, the youngest said, "Ah, we are still three days journey from home. I would that we could see our dear cousin, Nur al-Ninar, for the sight of whom, all these months I have been sick with longing."

"The wish is father to the deed," said Ali, and he held the magic glass to his brother's eye.

Then Ahmad turned pale and passed the glass to his brothers. "Alas," he said. "We have endured toil and hardship and traveled far, each hoping to wed our cousin, but all in vain, for I believe she is dying. I see her lying on her bed and around her, her women weep and lament. If you would see her one more time, take a final look through the glass." And the other two looked and it was so, and all three fell to weeping.

Then Ahmad said, "My brothers, we are all alike distracted with love for the princess. But I alone, if only I could reach her side in time, could save her and make her whole with the magical apple."

And Husayn said, "Only I can transport us to her side with the magic carpet."

And so, without further talk or delay, the three disposed themselves on the carpet and instantly Husayn willed them to the princess's bed chamber, where Ahmad, to the astonishment of her maid servants, held the apple to the nostrils of the dying princess. And when its fragrance reached her brain, the sickness left her. She opened her eyes, sat up in her bed, and seeing her cousins, held out her arms to them as joyfully as a child.

But how could the king decide which of the princes should wed her? Without the magical tube, the princes would not have known of their beloved's illness. Without the carpet they could not have reached her side in time. Without the apple they could not have cured her.

In his bafflement the king assigned the princes another test, a trial of bowmanship, and in this test Husayn, the eldest, carried off the prize, for he shot his arrow farthest. But Ahmad, who lost his arrow and so the match, came back the following day to find it and found, along with it, another adventure—with an enchanted castle and an evil witch and the fairy Peri Banu, whom after many more tests and trials and tales he wed and with whom he lived happily forever.

So the story goes, as Shahrazad, hostage night after night for the lives of every maiden in the kingdom, told it to the sultan.

But perhaps there is another tale, the tale of the three gifts, that Shahrazad told her sister Dunyazad in the idle hours of the afternoon, when they lingered in the garden, talking sadly, sometimes of their carefree childhood and sometimes of their friends who had died under the hand of the sultan's strangler.

In this tale the princess Nur has played all her life with her three cousins, each of whom, when she reaches womanhood wishes to make her his wife. As for Nur al-Ninar, she has come to love the youngest, who also loves her. When she is sixteen she learns, through one of her handmaidens who has overheard the sultan talking to his vizier, that she will be given in marriage to the eldest. She begs an audience with the sultan and persuades him that if she is given in marriage to Husayn, there will be rivalry among the three brothers and that in their rage and jealousy against the eldest, the two younger may plunge the kingdom into civil war. "Let me set the three a task," she says, "and wed the one whom I judge to have fulfilled it best. For what man would wed a woman who comes to him unwillingly or who regards him with scorn and finds secret ways to torment him and make his life miserable?"

Then the sultan agreed, for he knew well the misery a man may be put in by a vengeful woman and the chaos into which the kingdom may be thrown by warring princes.

So the princess called the three to her chamber and

directed them to set out into
the world and find, each one,
the gift that he believed would
most please her. And so they
went and traveled through the
world and returned in a year's
time, bearing gifts.

The eldest brought a bird—
the most beautiful bird in the
world. Its neck feathers of scarlet and gold glinted with spangles of iri-
descent blue and its tail of gold and green
and blue swept the floor behind its perch.
But its beauty was not the most intrigu-
ing thing about this bird. It spoke seven
languages and told amusing stories in
every one. And when it opened its beak, gold coins
fell into the cupped hands of the owner. The princess
looked upon the bird with delight and held in her
hand one of the golden coins. Then she turned to the
second brother, who had brought her a cat—no ordinary cat, but the loveliest cat in the world, with soft
fur and a soft purr and blue eyes with golden flecks in
them. But its beauty was not the most valuable thing
about the cat. For it had the gift of prophecy. Whatever the owner asked regarding the future, the prince
said, the cat would tell him. The princess looked upon
the cat with astonishment, and then she turned to
the third brother. "And what have you brought me,
Ahmad?" she said.

Then the youngest brother looked deep into the
princess Nur al-Ninar's eyes with all his love in his
face. "I have brought you this flower, beloved," he
said, "which I plucked by the roadside as I made
my way here this morning. For although I wandered
through all the world for a year and a day, dreaming of
your wit and beauty and your kindness and grace, I
found nothing that would be worthy of you. And so I

said to myself that perhaps we might give ourselves to each other and that such gifts would take a lifetime to deliver. So I bring you this flower in token of my thought. I see, though, that already the flower begins to droop, and I am sorry that I plucked it."

Then the princess held out her hand to Prince Ahmad and said that his gift pleased her above all things he might have brought her. And she said to Prince Husayn that doubtless with his bird he might woo the fairest princess in all Persia and that Prince Ali likewise should have no difficulty finding a bride. And so Ahmad and the Princess Nur al-Ninar were married, and although the prince did not succeed to the crown, he and his princess lived happily all their days.

But, so the story goes, although it is true that Prince Husayn found a beautiful wife, the unfortunate man was slain by robbers who came into his chamber at night, drawn by rumors about the bird from whose beak dropped golden coins. As for Prince Ali, he died young. It was said he died out of the fear of death. For his cat had prophesied that he would die young.

The Fisherman
and the Genie

S ire, said Shahrazad, there was once a poor man who dwelled by the sea—a humble man and a true worshipper of Allah. He had a wife and three daughters and he lived by casting his net into the sea and taking his catch to the market. It was his custom to cast his net only four times each day, for he said to himself that he would take his share of the fish in the sea and the rest he would leave to others whose need was as great as his.

One day, as was his custom, he went out at noon, set down his basket by the water and tucking up his shirt, waded in and made a cast. When his net had settled to the bottom, he gathered the cords and hauled away, but however hard he pulled, he could not bring it up. So he drew the cords together, drove a stake into the ground, and secured the net. Then he stripped, dived into the water, and worked the meshes this way and that to loosen them until he could drag it in. The net was torn and all he found inside was a dead jackass.

13

"There is no might save in Allah the Glorious," said the fisherman. And with that he pushed the body of the ass back into the sea, spread the net and mended it and cast it again, saying, "In Allah's name."

Again he found the net too heavy to pull in and when he had made it fast and stripped and gone deep into the water and pulled it loose and drawn it in, he found in it a huge earthen pitcher full of sand and mud. He threw the pitcher into the sea, spread his net and cast it again in Allah's name and waited until it sank. This time all he found inside were potsherds and broken glass.

Then, raising his eyes heavenward, the fisherman, said, "Ya, Allah, Thou knowest that I cast my net but four times each day, and now the third cast is drawn in and has brought me nothing. So this time, O my God, I pray thee, give me my daily bread," and calling once more on the name of God, he cast his net and waited as it sank and settled, and for the fourth time he could not haul it in for it was entangled at the bottom. Then he cried out in anger, "There is no Majesty and there is no might save in Allah!" But he could not help adding, "A curse be on this wretched world where I am overwhelmed by grief and misery." He stripped then and diving down to the net disentangled and drew it ashore.

When he loosened the cords and opened the meshes, he found inside a jar of brass shaped like a cucumber, heavy with its contents and stoppered with a leaden cap stamped with the seal ring of Solomon son of David. (Peace be to them both.) Seeing this, the fisherman was glad and said to himself, If I sell this brazen pot in the market it may be worth ten gold dinars. And who knows what treasure is inside.

Taking his knife, he worked at the lead until he had loosened the cap from the jar, and then he laid the cap on the ground and tilted the jar to pour out whatever might be inside. But nothing poured out. He weighed it again in his hands and it was as heavy as if it held a treasure of golden coins. He shook it and smoke began to drift out and trail along the ground and gather itself and spiral upward, until presently it seemed to condense and the terrified fisherman saw towering above him a genie, whose head touched the clouds even while his feet were on the ground.

His head was as big as the dome on the sultan's palace, his hands were like pitchforks, his legs were the trunks of cedar trees, his mouth like a cave with teeth as large as the tusks of elephants. His eyes were two lamps and his look fierce and glowing.

The fisherman shivered and his mouth was as dry as if it were filled with cotton wool. "There is no God but God," said the genie. "Be of good cheer, fisherman."

"Why should I be cheerful?" said the fisherman.

"Because of having to die an ill death this very hour," said the genie.

"What have I done to deserve death?" said the fisherman, "I, who drew thee out of the depths of the sea and freed thee from the jar."

"Ask me only what mode of death thou wouldst die and how I should slay thee."

Again the fisherman asked what he had done to deserve death and the genie said, "Hear my story, oh fisherman. Know that I was of the Ifrit, the schismatic Djinn, and that I rebelled against Solomon son of David (Peace be to them both) and the Prophet had his ministers seize me and bring me in chains before him and bade me swear obedience and when I refused, he shut me up in this jar and stopped it with a leaden seal on which he impressed the Most High Name and then he gave orders to cast me into the ocean, where I have lain these many hundred years. And at first I said to myself in the jar that whoever should release me, I would enrich him forever. But a century went by and when no one set me free, I said again, Whoever shall release me, to him I will open up the hoards of the earth. Still no one came and more hundreds of years passed. Then I said, I will grant to him who releases me three wishes. But still none came. Then, in my rage I said, From this time forth, whoever shall be so unfortunate as to set me free, him will I slay. But I will give him the choice of what death he will die. And now, fisherman, the choice is thine.''

And although the fisherman abased himself and begged for his life and called on Allah's name, saying, "Do not destroy me, lest God set over thee one who will destroy thee," the genie said only, "Enough of this foolish talk. Make your choice, for I will kill you."

Then the fisherman, who was not entirely devoid of mother wit, said, "Oh mighty one, if I must die I must die. But in the Most Great Name, graven on the seal ring of Solomon son of David (Peace be to both of them), if I ask thee one question, wilt thou give me a true answer?"

The Ifrit replied, "Yea," for hearing the mention of the Most Great Name, his wits were troubled and he shivered in all his smokiness. "Ask," he said, "and be brief."

Then the fisherman said, "Tell me how thou didst fit into this bottle which is not large enough, huge as it is, to hold thy hand. No, nor even thy finger. How came it to be large enough to contain the whole of thee?"

"What!" said the genie. "You doubt that I was in the jar?"

"I cannot believe it," said the fisherman, "for it is clearly impossible."

Then the genie smoked with rage and

blew himself up so that the top of his head touched the clouds.

"I'll never believe it," said the fisherman, "until I see it with my own eyes."

Then in an instant the genie shook and shrank and became a vapor which condensed, and little by little slipped into the jar until every wisp of him was inside.

Instantly the fisherman took up the leaden cap with the seal and stopped the mouth of the jar and called out to the Ifrit, saying, "Ask me by way of a boon what death thou wilt die." And he laughed, and then he said, "By Allah, I will throw thee into the sea, and here on the shore I'll build me a house and whoever comes, I'll warn him against fishing here and say, In these waters abides an Ifrit who gives as a favor to the man who saves him his choice of deaths."

The genie could think now of nothing but escape, of the awful fate of being back in the jar at the bottom of the sea, and he softened his voice and spoke as sweetly as if his smoky tongue dripped honey. "Oh, fisherman," he said, "open the jar and let me out and I will bring thee riches and good luck."

"If thou hadst spared me," said the fisherman, "I would spare thee. But nothing would satisfy thee save my death. So now I will hurl thee back into the sea."

"Nay, wait," said the genie. "Have mercy on me and pardon my past doings. As I have been tyrannous, be thou generous."

"Did I not say," said the fisherman, "'Do not destroy me, lest God set over thee one who will destroy thee?' And so it happened."

The Ifrit cried aloud then, and said, "I will make a covenant with thee, in the name of the Most High, and vow that I will never do thee hurt or harm. Rather will I help thee to what shall enrich thee and thine and free thee forever from the need to cast thy net into the sea." And he swore again in the name of the Most High.

Then the fisherman remembered how the genie had

trembled at Allah's name and, swearing him a third time with a solemn oath, opened the jar. The pillar of smoke again rose until it was fully out and thickened and became the Ifrit of hideous countenance who instantly gave the bottle such a kick that it flew far up and fell into the ocean. And the fisherman doubted his wisdom, saying to himself, This business promiseth badly. But then he put on a brave face and spoke. "Oh, Ifrit, in the name of God, fulfill thy oath and do not play me false. Spare me, so that Allah may spare thee."

The Ifrit turned and stalked away, saying, "Follow me, then, and bring thy net."

And the fisherman, not yet sure of his own safety, followed at a considerable distance. They passed through the outskirts of the city and through a wilderness to the side of a mountain lake as still and blue as the sky, and the Ifrit waded into the middle and again called, "Follow me."

Then he bade the fisherman cast his net, and when the fisherman looked into the water, he was astonished to see schools of fish of four colors: white and red and blue and yellow. He cast his net and hauled it in and saw that he had netted four fish, one of each color.

"Carry these to the sultan," said the Ifrit, "and set them in his presence and he will give thee what shall make thee a wealthy man. And now," he added, bowing his smokiness low, "accept my excuses, for I would go, having lain in the sea eighteen hundred years and not seen the face of the world until this hour." And he gave the fisherman godspeed and struck the earth with one foot, and the ground split open and swallowed him up.

The fisherman, marvelling at all that had happened, took the fish home and filled an earthen bowl with water and bore them off splashing and wriggling to the palace. There he laid the fish before the king, who wondered exceedingly at the sight, for he had never seen fish like this, all glittering gold and blue and red as the clouds at sunset and white as the noon sky and graceful in form as mermaids. He commanded his wazir to give the fisherman four hundred dinars.

And the fisherman took the coins and gave thanks to Allah's name and ran off home stumbling and falling and rising again and deeming the whole thing to be a dream. The gold, however, was pure and real, and with it he bought for his family all they needed and wanted, and he went in that night to his wife in joy and gladness.

So much concerning the fisherman. As for the many-colored fish and how they came to be in the lake, and what happened to them and to the king and how they led him to a far country and a great adventure, that's a tale for another night.

Sindbad and the Roc

Long ago in the city of Baghdad, said Shahrazad, there lived a wealthy merchant, Sindbad, who had traveled over all the world by land and sea and had suffered hardships and privation, found and lost fortunes in jewels and spices many times over. And every evening, when the sun set beyond his garden and the fountain splashed softly in the courtyard, it was his custom to gather his friends about him and entertain them with wine and sweet music and tales of adventures.

I had wearied of ease, my brothers (he began his tale one evening), and longed for adventure and I resolved one day to travel again to far-away lands and gain my living by trading in silks and other precious goods such as the world prizes. I rose and went into the market place and bought merchandise suited to my purpose and packed up the bales and departed from Baghdad for the city of Bassorah where I bought a tall ship and hired a master and crew. I set over them my slaves and pages as superintendents and, in the company of merchants who had stowed their bales in my ship and paid me hire, put out to sea.

We traveled together from island to island and sea to sea, buying and selling and diverting ourselves with the customs of strange cities until we arrived one day at a desolate island where we saw no man and no habitation save for one enormous white dome half-buried in the sand. We were curious and beached the ship, and some among the merchants and crew set out to examine this dome and discover what it was. But I stayed behind in the ship.

Presently one of my servants came running and called out to me, "Master, arise and divert thyself with the sight of this egg which we imagined to be a dome."

I rose and went ashore and there found that the party of merchants, seeing what they believed to be an egg, were striking it with stones to discover what was inside.

When I saw what they were doing, I was filled with horror and called out to them in haste, "In the name of Allah, do not this deed, for this must be the egg of the great Roc, who will come and demolish our ship and destroy us." They would not hear my words but continued to strike the egg and when it broke, there poured out a flood of liquid and a young bird was moving inside. So they pulled it out and killed it and took from it a quantity of meat.

And while I was watching, the day darkened and a cloud obscured the whole sky. I looked up to see if a storm might be coming and saw that the wings of the Roc, flying high above us, were shading us from the sun's light. And the Roc, when she saw the egg broken and her chick dead, gave a shriek that made the trees bend, and then her mate came and they flew in circles over us crying out with cries louder than thunder.

So I called to the master and sailors to put to sea and seek safety before we perished. We hastened aboard, and the master cast off and put on all sail. When the Rocs saw this, they flew away and we thought we might escape them. But then, again, the sky darkened and now they flew over us and their wing beats made the waves heave as if there were a hurricane and, looking up, I saw that each one had a stone in its claws and beat its wings heavily, hardly able to stay aloft with such a burden. The male bird flew over us and dropped his stone. But the master, anticipating his direction, steered hard a-port and the stone missed us by a little space. When it struck the water, it made such a wave that the ship was carried up, up, and then dropped down until we saw the floor of the sea. Then the female dropped her stone and, as fate would have it, it fell on the stern of the ship and crushed it, and the ship took on water and sank.

I strove to save myself, and God, whose name be exalted, placed in my reach a floating spar, and I caught hold of it. Wind and waves carried me forward, so that by the permission of God I drifted at last to an island and washed up on a desolate beach, half-dead with hunger and thirst and exhaustion. For a long while I lay on the sand, scarcely able to move. When at last I rose and walked along the shore, I saw that the island was like the gardens of Paradise. Fig trees bent down their branches, heavy with fruit, and on the hillsides olives grew. Rocks green as malachite and black as obsidian sparkled under the sun, and briar bushes scattered among them were heavy with ripe berries. I ate the fruit and drank from the river and praised God whose name be exalted and glorified.

But still I heard not a single voice, nor did I see any man. And I was like a dead man from fatigue and fear and lay down again and slept until morning, when I rose and walked among the trees and, approaching a narrow stream, saw an old man, clothed from the waist down in a garment made of leaves. So I said to myself, perhaps this old man is one of our company who was shipwrecked. I approached and greeted him, and he greeted me with a sign, not speaking.

Then I spoke to him again, asking what he did there, but still he said nothing; only standing up, as it seemed, feebly and with great difficulty, he made signs that he wished me to carry him across the stream to gather some fruit. I took him up on my shoulders and forded the stream which was nowhere more than waist deep, but when on the other side I made to put him down, he wrapped his legs about my chest and locked his ankles and held me in such a grip that I thought I might suffocate. Indeed I was so overcome with fear that I fell to the ground and afterwards (I know not how long I lay there insensible) roused and staggered to my feet, trying vainly to dislodge him. He seized me by the hair and made it clear that I must take him under the trees, where he gathered and ate the golden pears and ripe plums that hung down everywhere. Thus he rode me as if I were his donkey all day and even at night, when I fell to the ground exhausted, he did not let go his grip. So, filled with rage and hatred, I carried him for days, plotting every moment how I might trick him.

One day as he slept (still holding me as tightly as if his legs were steel bands) I saw nearby some dry gourds and hanging just within reach a grape vine laden with ripe grapes, and instantly I knew the means of my release. Cautiously, without rousing him, I squeezed a quantity of grapes into the gourds, and left them hidden under the vines. A few days later, when he made signs to me to lie down in the same place, I took up a gourd and drank, and the draft was an excellent wine, so strong that it tempted me to dance and sing and forget my horrid burden. When he saw me drinking, he tightened his legs like a vise around my chest and made signs that I should give him the gourd, but I pretended that I would drain it and give him none. He snatched it away from me then and drank his fill, and I contrived it so that he saw the other gourds in the shade of the vine and he took them up and drank from them, too. Not many minutes passed before his head drooped and I began to feel the iron grip of his legs relaxing and his hands slipping loose from my hair. With a mighty heave I threw him to the ground and ran leaping and singing and shouting along the sea shore, filled with joy at my escape, rejoicing in the sea breeze.

And I bathed in the waters and feasted on apples and olives and continued on my way until, the third day, I met a party of seamen whose captain received me kindly and heard with amazement my strange tale. I set sail, then, with this kind man, and that night we made port in a safe harbor where I met with an even stranger adventure. But the fire burns low, my friends, and it is late. That tale is for another night.

Rapunzel

There was once a pregnant woman who lived next door to a witch, of whom she and her husband were thoroughly afraid— a skinny old crone with sharp teeth and a long chin with a black mole that had three hairs growing in it. Greatly fearing that the witch might do them some mischief, the two had always kept to their own house and scarcely even looked in the direction of the witch's house. But one day when the woman was standing in the window of her bedroom, she chanced to glance over the wall into the witch's garden and saw growing there a fine crop of lettuce. The poor woman was seized with such a longing for a lettuce salad that she almost fainted, and she begged her husband to climb over the wall and steal a handful for her. He was afraid, for he knew the witch's evil reputation, but at last he yielded to his wife's pleading and climbed over the wall and hastily pulled up a handful and brought it home.

But his wife was not satisfied with one salad and the next day she begged him to go again and steal her lettuce, and he did. This time the witch noticed that someone had been trampling her garden and determined to conceal herself under the ground with only one ear sticking out so as to hear the approach of the thief and surprise him, whoever he might be.

That night, however, when the wife begged her husband to go again for lettuce, he refused.

"Very well," said his wife, "if you won't go, I will have to go myself," and over the wall she went. Just as she was about to pull a handful of curly green lettuce, she spied the witch's ear sticking out of the ground. "Ah," she said, "here's an excellent mushroom. I'll just take it home for supper along with the lettuce." And she seized the ear and gave a pull.

Out popped the witch with a horrible shriek that frightened the poor wife out of her wits.

"Thief!" screamed the witch, "Stealing my rapunzel" (For that was what lettuce was called in that country.) "I'll pinch off your nose with red hot pincers and I may even eat you for supper."

The terrified wife begged and pled and told the witch of her pregnancy, which had made her yearn so after the lettuce. At last the witch said, "Very well, then. It's not the child's fault you're so greedy. I shall let you take as much lettuce as you like. But you must promise when the child is twelve years old to give it to me."

In her fright, the wife agreed. She took the lettuce and went home and ate it happily and put the whole matter out of her mind, saying to herself that twelve years was a long time and surely the witch would forget.

When the child, a little daughter, was born, she named her Rapunzel.

Rapunzel thrived and grew and soon she was a tall and beautiful young girl with golden hair so long that if it was not plaited and wound round her head, it trailed on the ground behind her.

One day when she was almost twelve years old, Rapunzel, on her way to school, met a strange-looking old woman with black teeth and a long chin, who stopped in the roadway and spoke to her. "Child," said the old woman, "tell your mother to bring me what she has promised."

But Rapunzel went on her way and forgot the old woman's words.

Twice more the witch reminded her, saying, "Child, tell your mother to bring me what she promised." And the third time she bit the girl on the arm with her black teeth until it bled and cried, "This is so you won't forget my orders."

Rapunzel ran home and told her mother about the wicked old woman. The mother bandaged her daughter's arm, looked at her sadly, and said to herself, It cannot be helped. And to Rapunzel she said, "Tell her then to take what she was promised where she finds it."

When Rapunzel delivered this answer, the witch seized her by her long hair and led her, as one leads a lamb, far away to a tower she had built in the woods, a tall tower with no steps leading to the top and with no doors and only a window through which Rapunzel could see the surrounding forest, the flying birds and the blue sky. There the witch kept her a prisoner, and when she wanted to get in, she stood under the tower and called out, "Rapunzel, Rapunzel, let down thy hair," and climbed up as nimbly as if the braids were a ladder.

Three long years Rapunzel spent in the tower. Every day the witch came to visit her and bring her food and drink and to admire her beauty. Since Rapunzel was a clever girl, she never missed an opportunity to observe the witch and question her, saying, Grandmother, teach me this or that, for I see how clever you are and I wish to be like you. Thus she soon began to master the witch's magic.

One day, after three years had passed, it happened that a young prince who was hunting in the forest passed close to the tower and saw Rapunzel standing in her window singing and brushing out her hair. She sang so sweetly that the prince fell in love with her at once. But since there was no door to the tower and no stairway or ladder, he despaired of reaching her. Still, after that day, he went to the forest again and again and made his way to the tower and listened to her songs. One day, as he was standing concealed in the shadowy wood, he saw the witch come down the path and call, "Rapunzel, Rapunzel, let down thy hair."

Now he saw how he might enter the tower, and when it was dark, he came out of the wood and called softly, "Rapunzel, Rapunzel, let down thy hair."

And she, thinking it was the witch, let down her hair, not braided now, but flowing like a golden waterfall, and drew him up.

She was startled but not frightened when she saw him. She had not seen a human being for three long years—not a single human creature except the witch with her long chin and black mole. But the prince was so fair and had such a smile that she could not think he meant her harm. "Who are you and what do you want of me?" she said. She looked at him admiringly. "I have not seen a man since I left my father's house," she said. "How handsome you are."

"Not nearly so handsome as you are fair," said the prince, and he took her hand and told her how he had watched her and listened to her sing and they fell to talking and talked all night long. The prince charmed her with his manners and sang her a song as beautiful as any she could sing. In no time at all she had fallen in love with him. Every night he came to see her, and before dawn she let down her hair and he went on his way. On his third visit they agreed to be married and planned together how they would escape.

"Each night, when you come," Rapunzel said, "bring a skein of silk with you. I will braid a ladder and, when it is finished, I will climb down to you and we'll ride far away where the witch will never find us."

And so, each night, the prince brought a skein of silk, and at last the night came when the ladder was finished, and the prince rode up to the tower and Rapunzel prepared to climb down.

But the witch, who had observed how happy Rapunzel was lately, how she was always singing in the tower and no longer seemed restless and discontented nor asked questions about the outside world, was suspicious, and that night she came to the tower to see if anything was amiss.

Fortunately Rapunzel had observed the witch's suspicious glances and prepared herself. Now, before she climbed down from the tower, she put into her pocket three balls of yarn: one green, one blue, and one red, over which, using the spells the witch had taught her, she had said certain words.

Just as the prince took Rapunzel up on his horse to ride away, the witch ran out of the woods with a terrible scream of rage and stepped into their path. The prince spurred his horse who gave a mighty leap right over the witch's head and galloped away.

"We will never escape, dear Rapunzel," the prince said, for he had looked back and seen that the witch was in close pursuit and was gaining on them.

But then Rapunzel took the green ball from her pocket and dropped it in front of the witch. Immediately a garden sprang up and in it a lettuce patch where the gardener was chopping weeds.

The witch, beside herself with rage, shouted at him, "Gardener, did you see a youth and maiden riding this way?"

"Eh?" the gardener said, and cupped his hand to his ear, for he was deaf.

"A couple. A girl with long hair."

"A couple of pears?" said the gardener. "Yes, the pears are fine this year. Do have one. Or even two."

"No, no. A girl on a horse who passed in the lane."

"Ah, purslane. Yes, it makes a fine salad," said the gardener.

"Toward the east, you fool. Toward the rising sun."

"You're right. The vegetables must have sun," the gardener said.

The witch lost patience then and ran on, and soon she was gaining on the couple again. But Rapunzel threw down the ball of blue yarn and a great lake flowed across the witch's path with a fisherman standing on the shore by his boat.

"Quick, quick, take me across," screamed the witch.

"What's the hurry, old lady?" the fisherman said. "The other side will be there tomorrow."

Then she fetched him a blow on the head with her umbrella that knocked him silly.

"Take yourself, then," muttered the fisherman and with that he ran away as fast as his legs would carry him.

The witch jumped in the boat and rowed and rowed, and at last she reached the other side and set off again.

Soon she saw the prince and Rapunzel in the distance riding the prince's white mare, Rapunzel's hair flying out behind her like a cloud of spun gold.

"Oh, I'll have you yet," she muttered.

But then Rapunzel looked back and threw down the last ball of yarn, the red one, and immediately a wall of flame sprang up. The witch was running so fast that she ran right into the fire and was burnt to a cinder.

The prince and Rapunzel rode on to his kingdom where they were received with rejoicing and married and lived happily for the rest of their lives.

The Six Swans

One cold winter afternoon the king of a certain country, while he was hunting in the forest, gave chase to a great stag and rode so fast and so far into the forest that he left all his men behind him. At last, looking about him, he saw that he was lost. He rode this way and that, searching for a way out, but the forest lay under the spell of a witch, and the farther he rode, the more hopelessly lost he was. Finally he stumbled on a path and followed it to a clearing where he saw a house with an old woman sitting on the doorstep, as comfortably as if it were summertime. He dismounted and spoke courteously to her and asked if she could show him the way out of the woods.

"Indeed I can, oh King," she said. "I can and I alone." (For she was the witch of the wood.) "But there is a condition and unless you consent to it, you will wander in these woods until you die."

When the king asked what the condition was, the witch answered him by saying, "I have a daughter, fair as any in your land and worthy to be a queen. If you wish to return to your kingdom, you must make her your wife."

Then she took him into the house and showed him her daughter who was as beautiful as the witch had said, with black hair coiled in a braid around her head and narrow green eyes and lips and cheeks so red it was as if one could see the blood throbbing under her skin. Yes, she was beautiful, but, when he drew near, it seemed to him that her smile was as cold as the north wind. He could scarcely look at her without a shudder. Nevertheless, having little choice in the matter, he pledged his word and took her up before him on the saddle. She touched his horse's neck with her cold hand and said, "Give him his head, my lord," and they found their way without difficulty to his royal palace where they were wed.

Now the king had been married before and he had by his first wife six sons and a daughter whom he loved better than life, and he feared that this new wife of his with her narrow eyes and cold hand would do them some harm, so he took them away to a lonely tower hidden in the woods where he believed they would be safe. Indeed this place was so well hidden that he himself could not have found it if he had not had a magic ball of yarn which, when he threw it down before him, unwound itself and showed him the way.

Every day the king set out to the forest to visit his children and soon the queen, who saw him depart and return with never a word as to where he had been, grew curious. She gave a purse full of silver to one of his servants and at the same time passed her hand before his eyes and he then disclosed the secret and told her also of the ball of yarn which alone could show the way.

Secretly she watched until she discovered where the king hid the ball of yarn. Then she set to work and wove seven silken shirts and, as she worked, she wove into them a powerful spell. One day, when the king was away, she took the shirts and set the magic ball of yarn rolling and followed it into the forest. The brothers, who saw the ball rolling toward them, thought their father was coming and ran joyfully to meet him. Then over each one the queen threw one of the shirts and the six were instantly turned into swans and, lifting their white wings, flew high into the air and disappeared. The queen, in her haste to get back to the palace before her absence was discovered, did not stop to find the sister, but said to herself that she would come back another day and deal with her.

When the king came next day to the tower, his daughter ran out to greet him and told him how her brothers had vanished and how she had seen six swans flying above the treetops and circling and calling to her. Then the king grieved for his sons and said to his daughter that he must take her even farther away to some place where she would be safe, but she begged him to let her stay one more night in the forest tower. "For," she said, "perhaps my brothers will return, after all." When the king was gone, however, she said to herself that she could not stay a minute longer alone in the place where she and her brothers had spent so many happy hours together and she set out in the darkness to look for them. Calling their names and weeping, she walked all night and all the next day, until she was so weary she could not take another step, and then, as the sun was setting, she made a nest of leaves under a great oak tree and lay down to rest.

Just as the sun disappeared below the horizon, she heard a rustle of wings and six beautiful white birds

flew down into the clearing
and lit around her. The breeze
stirred and lifted their feathers and before her eyes the
feathers dropped away and
there were her brothers. She sprang up and they
embraced and kissed her and told her how
their stepmother had enchanted them and how
they had been watching over her wanderings.

"Oh, please," said the princess, "let me stay
with you, for I am lonely and have no place
to turn."

"No," said the eldest. "It's impossible. We are allowed to shed our swan feathers only once each day,
for fifteen minutes in the evening just at sunset. Afterwards we become swans again and must fly away."

"Is there no way I can help you break this terrible
spell?" said the princess.

"Ah, there is," said the eldest brother, "but it is too
difficult. We cannot bear to tell you."

Still she begged and at last they told her how the
spell could be broken. She must not speak or laugh
for six long years, they said, and during that time she
must gather thistles and card and spin them into
thread and weave them into cloth and make six shirts.
"And when they are made," said the eldest, "if you
throw them over us, the spell will be broken. But unless the work is finished within six years, we must stay
swans forever."

Fifteen minutes had passed since the brothers had
flown down and shed their swan feathers, and now,
swans again, they lifted their great wings with lonely
cries of farewell, and flew away into the gathering
darkness.

Their sister resolved to set to work that very night.
She made her way deeper into the forest and gathered
thistles and climbed into the crotch of a low-growing
tree and, after she had slept, began to card and spin the

thread and to weave the cloth for her brothers' shirts. Her hands were blistered and burned from handling the fiery thistles, but still she worked on. She had no one to talk to and no wish to laugh, so month after month she sat in her tree spinning the thread and weaving the cloth.

After many months had passed, the king of that country, who happened to be returning from a festival in a neighboring country, passed under the tree where she sat and, chancing to look up, saw her there.

"Who are you, lovely lady?" he called out. "And what are you doing sitting in a tree in the middle of the woods?" For although her clothes were tattered by now and her hair tangled, still she was as beautiful as the morning.

She shook her head when the king spoke and kept on with her work and said nothing.

"Come down," he said. "Come down. No one will hurt you."

Again she shook her head. No matter how gently he coaxed her, she would not come down. So he or-dered his men to climb up into the tree and bring her down. She gathered her thistles and cloth and came, weeping.

The king took her up before him on his saddle and put his cloak about her. He questioned her again, but still she only shook her head and looked at him so sadly that his heart was moved. He took her back with him to his castle and there he had fine clothes made for her and placed her beside him at the table.

As time passed, her gentleness and modest ways pleased the king more and more, and in the course of time he asked her if she would be his wife. The princess said to herself that he was so kind she could not help loving him and, although she still said not a word, she nodded her head, *Yes,* and they were wed.

But still, secretly, at night, she left the palace and along the roadside gathered thistles and brought them back and in her private chamber continued to work on the shirts that would free her brothers.

Now the king's mother, who was a wicked woman, was jealous of his love for his silent wife, and she never let pass the chance to try to insinuate into his mind doubts about her—saying that she was lowborn or that she must be a witch and that there could be none but an evil reason for her silence. But the king paid no attention.

In time, when the queen bore a son, the king's mother came secretly in the night and smeared her mouth with blood and took away the child. Then she went to the king and said that his wife was a cannibal and had killed and eaten the child. The king grieved for his son, but he could not believe ill of his gentle wife and so he protected her from harm. When a second child came, his mother did the same thing and accused her again. And with the third, a little daughter, even the king could not protect his wife from judgment. The king's mother spread her tales and the people demanded that the queen be turned over to the court for trial. There she was condemned to be burned as a witch.

All this time, she had uttered no word in her own defense and, although her tears had fallen as she grieved for her children, still, at night, she spun and wove and cut and sewed for her brothers.

Now it was the last day of the six years of her vow.

The soldiers put her in a cart and dragged her through the streets to the place of execution. Still she worked, for she had finished all the shirts save one, and it lacked only a sleeve. As she worked, they brought her to the stake and piled up wood and straw around her and lit the fire and the smoke whirled upward. All the while, as she continued to sew, the queen turned and turned her head, looking toward the horizon in every direction.

Suddenly, as she looked, out of the sky flew down six great white swans. With huge wing beats they scattered the wood, and the wind of their flying put out the fire. Their sister took the six shirts and threw one over each swan and all stood up and were men. Only the sixth had a wing for a left arm because his sister had not finished the last sleeve of his shirt.

Then the princess, released from her vow, went to the king, who was speechless with astonishment, and said to him, "Now, dear husband, I can speak, for I have freed my brothers from this wicked spell. I am innocent of my children's blood," she said. "Never, never would I have harmed them."

And when the king made inquiries, he discovered where they were hidden and his anger against his mother was so great that he would have had her brought to the stake and burned in his wife's place, but that she had heard his servants approaching and took the form of a black raven and flew away out the palace window and was never seen again.

But the king and queen were reunited with their children and together with her six brothers lived many years in peace and happiness.

Thumbelina

Once upon a time there was a woman who longed to have a child but who had no husband. At last, in despair, she went to an old witch and asked her help. "I would so like to have a child," she said. "Perhaps you can help me get one."

"No trouble at all," said the witch. "Take this grain of corn and plant it in a pot. It's a very special kind of corn. Plant it and water it and see what happens."

The woman did as the witch had told her and planted the corn and set the pot in the window. Next morning when she looked, a beautiful plant had sprung up with dark green leaves and silky golden tassels. It was indeed a special kind of corn plant, for it had not only tasseled corn on it, but a beautiful cornflower, which as she watched opened its petals to the sunshine. There in its center sat a tiny maiden not half so big as your thumb with hair the color of corn tassels and eyes as blue as the petals of the cornflower.

The woman took her up gently and put her on the table by the kitchen window. There she made a cozy

room and a playground for her. She set around her a
tiny screen all painted with castles and fountains and
fairies and inside she put a polished walnut shell for a
bed and filled it with thistledown and made a coverlet
of silk. And she fashioned a washbowl of an acorn cup
and of another a chair with a puff ball inside for a
cushion. For her amusement she made a harp of twigs
strung with spider's silk and outside the screen she set
a soup bowl and filled it with water and put in a milkweed pod for a boat. All day long Thumbelina (for so
her mother named her) sang to the music of her harp
and when she tired of that she swam in her pool or
poled her milkweed pod with a sturdy broomstraw.

But one night while she lay sleeping, a fat yellow
toad hopped through the window onto her table and,
seeing her lying there, said, "Ah, what a pretty creature! I'll take her home to be a wife for my son." And
taking the shell with Thumbelina in it, she hopped
through the window and back to the swampy edge of

the stream where she lived with her son, a sluggish green and yellow spotted fellow who had a wide mouth which he opened only once in a while to shoot out his slimy tongue for a fly or, in the spring time, to croak "Knee deep and deeper," as if no one knew how deep the marsh was.

"Here is a bride for you, my son," said his mother, and showed him Thumbelina sleeping in her shell.

"Belly deep," said the son.

"We'll put her on a lily pad while we prepare a home in the mud for the two of you," said the mother, and they did. Next morning, Thumbelina awoke and found herself marooned on a lily pad growing in the stream that flowed through the marsh. The current tugged at the lily pad and the leaf shook and Thumbelina was afraid—but not so afraid as she was when the frog son and his mother came and told her what was to be her fate. The son shot out his tongue and caught a fly and offered it to her and when she declined, he

ate it himself and said, "Belly deep." Then they took
away her polished bed to her new home, saying that
they would be back for her when all was ready.

Thumbelina wept and felt the lily pad rock under
her and looked around to see if there was any way she
might escape. Gazing down into the water, she saw
minnows swimming and nibbling at a floating leaf.

"Oh, fish, dear fish," she called out. "Please, can
you help me escape from this pad?"

The fish had heard all that had passed between
Thumbelina and the toads, of whom they were not the
least fond, and when Thumbelina cried out to them
for help, they swam under the lily pad and nibbled
through its stem, and in a moment it was carried out
into the stream and floated away.

On either side of the stream willow trees bent their
heads and red-winged blackbirds swung on the cat-
tails and gave their trilling cries. The pad floated on
for a long time until the water began to turn salty and
Thumbelina saw crabs scuttling along in the sand and
feared that she might be carried out to sea. Just then a
butterfly, all plum-colored and blue and black, flew
down and lit beside her and she gently stroked his
feathery wings and sang to him so sweetly that he
continued to fly round and round her and at last,
when he lit again, she took her girdle and tied it
lightly about him, thinking that she might persuade
him to fly toward the shore and draw her pad into a
safe harbor. For, although she had learned to swim in
her plate at home, the current of the stream was so
strong and the twigs, which were as big as logs to her,
whirled by so fast, she knew she could not escape by
swimming. But just as she had secured the butterfly
with her sash, a great stag beetle with a shiny black
back and fierce nippers swooped down and snatched
her up and flew up into a nearby tree, where he set her
down and looked her over.

Thumbelina saw her lily pad raft swept on down the

swift stream toward the sea and called out to the butterfly, of whom she had got quite fond, and she saw him beat his wings and lift himself into the air with her sash trailing behind him, but as to what happened to him afterwards, she never knew.

Then the beetle said to Thumbelina that she was very pretty and brought her a drop of nectar from a honeysuckle vine and considered whether he would make her his wife. But the lady stag beetles gathered around and looked at her and said what a poor thin ugly creature she was and with her soft white skin and only two legs. "Why," they said, "if she wasn't so small we would think she was one of those monstrous humans that come crashing through the woods and, if we're not quick, trample us and crush our beautiful shiny exo-skeletons." So the stag beetle agreed with them that Thumbelina was a pitiful-looking creature and flew off without another word.

Then Thumbelina climbed down from the tree, whose bark was so rough that she could easily find a footing, like a mountain climber, in its cracks and crevices.

Although she was alone again and very lonely, Thumbelina set about doing what she could for herself. She made a hammock of woven grasses and slung it under a fern leaf and made a coverlet of flower petals. And she made a bowl from an acorn cup, remembering the one her mother had given her, and each morning filled it with sparkling dewdrops so that she would have water to drink all day. Thus she lived all summer among the flowers, sipping nectar from honeysuckle and trumpet vine and wild clematis and nibbling at kernels of corn that fell from the plants in a field nearby and eating sweet carrot greens.

But fall came and the weather changed. The flowers withered. One night there was a heavy frost and she woke to find her fern all shriveled and yellow and her coverlet sparkling with ice crystals. By now her clothes were in rags and the cold wind struck through them. Thumbelina knew that if she did not find shelter she would die.

All summer she had seen the field mice scurrying through the corn field and had often spoken with them, although they had not much time for her. Now she wondered if she might beg shelter from them, and she made her way through a tunnel in the grass from which she'd often seen them slip out into the corn field. Soon she came to a little hollow in a fence post where a grandmotherly old mouse lived and knocked on her door. When the old mouse saw the shivering maiden on her doorstep, she took her in and sat her down by the warm fire and fed her broth and cornbread. "You poor child," she said. "Have you taken no thought all this long summer for what would happen to you in the winter? How impractical you are! But never mind. I have grain and nuts enough for both of us. You may stay with me over the winter and earn your keep by tidying my house and telling me stories in the long winter evenings. And if you can't make plans for your future, perhaps I can take you in hand and make them for you."

That very day the mouse's friend, a wealthy mole who had his quarters close by, stopped in to call. ("Be respectful," the mouse whispered hastily to Thumbelina when she saw him coming. "For he is quite wealthy and a pillar of the community.") And she had Thumbelina sing for him and tell him a fairy tale that her mother had told her. The mole was captivated, for although he was blind and could not see how lovely she was, he delighted in stories and sweet music.

The next day he invited Thumbelina and the field mouse to visit him in his tunnels, and for their convenience he dug a fresh connection between his quarters and theirs. From this he emerged into the mouse's cozy kitchen, sneezing and wiggling his sharp nose and smelling of roots and rotting leaves. He blinked his brown slits of eyes, with which he saw nothing, and bowed ceremoniously. The mouse seized a brush and brushed off his velvet coat, and then the three made their way toward his home.

"Unfortunately," he said, "we will have to pass by the body of a dead bird which had the temerity to fall through the roof just as I was digging toward your lovely cottage. Silly creature. He doubtless stayed too long after the end of summer and froze to death for his folly."

When they came to the place in the tunnel where the bird lay, Thumbelina saw that it was a hummingbird, its throat all ruby and its green neck feathers glinting under the light of the mouse's torch. Then, while the mole and the mouse talked of their storehouses, she smoothed down its feathers and thought to herself that perhaps she, too, might have ended thus.

That night she lay down in her little room, but she could not sleep for thinking of the poor bird and, slipping out of bed, she made a coverlet of woven grasses, thinking to give it a proper burial. Then she took the mouse's torch and made her way through the tunnel to where the bird lay, half-covered now with dirt, for the mole had begun to cover its body and intended to change the course of the tunnel to avoid the grave.

Thumbelina dragged the poor bird into a side tunnel, talking all the while. "Poor bird," she said, "sleep quietly here and dream of summer." She laid her head against its soft breast and heard a faint heartbeat and knew the bird was alive. Then she brushed away the dirt and laid the coverlet over him and brought thistledown and spread it around him and a bowl of water with a few drops of honey in it and lifted his head, and feebly the bird opened his bill and sipped from her cup.

She said nothing to the mouse, but the next night

came again and found the bird still living, but so weak it could barely whisper its thanks. "When I am a bit stronger," whispered the bird, "I will fly away to the south."

"Oh no," said Thumbelina. "Snow has fallen and the north wind blows. Stay here under my warm coverlet and I will take care of you." And so she did, bringing sugar water and honey each day when the mouse was napping. And the two grew fond of each other.

As for the mole, he had made a new tunnel and forgotten the bird, which was a creature for whom he had nothing but contempt.

The months passed and when spring came and the sun warmed the earth and brought flowers to the Cherokee roses and the hedgerows, Thumbelina guided the humming bird through the mole's tunnels and out into the sunshine, where he leapt into the air and, flashing all green and scarlet in the light, hovered over Thumbelina's head. "Climb on my back and fly with me into the green wood," he begged. But Thumbelina knew that the old field mouse would be distressed if she left her, and she shook her head.

"Farewell, then, sweet maiden," said the bird and flew away.

Then Thumbelina wept a little and returned to the home of the old field mouse where she tidied up the kitchen and looked out into the cornfield and said that perhaps she should go and gather dandelion greens for their supper. But the mouse said to her, "No, my dear, for you have other and more important fish to fry. All your singing and story telling this winter has served you well. The mole came to me this morning and asked for your hand in marriage. So you must stay at home and spin and weave and prepare your wedding clothes and the bed and table linens for your new home. I shall hire the three garden spiders who live in the cornfield to spin silks for your trousseau, and I myself will gather cotton wool when the bolls open to stuff your mattresses and make your coverlets."

So Thumbelina was obliged to sit and spin, and each evening the mole came snuffling through the tunnel and shook the dust from his velvet coat and squinted his blind eyes and sat and listened to her sing and tell tales of princes and palaces and far away lands. "It's all very well to tell stories of such matters," he said, "but, as you know, you will be far more comfortable with me in my underground house than you could ever be in a drafty palace with the wind blowing through all the windows."

Fall came and the date of the wedding was set in three weeks' time.

Still Thumbelina had not the heart to tell the mole that she could not love him, or to disappoint the expectations of the mouse who had been so kind to her.

Each morning, though, she slipped out to the end of the mouse's grass run in the corn field and watched the corn blowing in the wind and the clouds passing across the blue sky. Always she hoped that she might catch a glimpse of her hummingbird and know that he was still alive.

All around her the fall flowers nodded, great sunflowers high above her head and tiny blue asters and butterfly weed and fall daisies. Thumbelina wept to know that she would soon be living underground shut away forever from the green wood and the bright fields. She held up her arms to the wind and cried out her farewell to the light of the sun. "If you see my hummingbird," she said to the sunflowers, "greet him for me."

Then, all of a sudden she saw a flash of green light

from whirring wings and a patch of ruby breast, and there he was hovering in the air above her. "Thumbelina," he cried, "I have come to ask you one last time to come away with me. Fly with me to the warm south where winter never shrivels the green leaves and the breeze is as soft as the thistledown with which you warmed me. Come away. Your destiny can never be to live in the dark earth among moles and mice."

Thumbelina looked back through the grass run toward the mouse's dark home, and thought of the mole and his dusty coat and his hoards of buried wealth. "I will come," she said.

The tiny bird hovered in the air at her side and she slipped up onto his back and buried herself in his soft feathers, and they flew away together over wide fields and glinting sea waves and high snow-covered mountains where the air was so cold that Thumbelina shivered in her feathery nest.

They came at last to the warm countries where jacaranda trees waved their scarlet heads in the wind and acacias spread their limbs over shaded courtyards, where fountains murmured under orange trees and avocado trees heavy with ripe fruit, and in the fields butterflies were like showers of gold. "Here is my summer home," said the bird, and he hovered above the field and then set Thumbelina down on the branch of a tree where sprays of orchids drooped and cascaded to the ground. Then he flew off to find a mate and build a nest.

There, on a broad leaf—amazing—Thumbelina saw a little man all dressed in a green suit, his skin as brown from sunshine as an acorn. And he had a pair of fine wings folded on his shoulders and on his head a crown of gold, for in that country a little man or woman very much like him lived in every flower, and he was king of the flower people.

"How small you are," whispered Thumbelina, for

of course she had never seen people who were as small as she.

The king thought Thumbelina the loveliest maiden he had ever seen. He bowed before her and then called together his people and they brought her robes of flower petals and appointed a flower to be her home and, best of all, brought a pair of rose-colored wings and fastened them to her shoulders so that she, too, could fly like a butterfly from flower to flower.

The king of the flower people said that, with her permission, Thumbelina should be called Maia now. "For," he said, "Thumbelina is such an ugly name I cannot imagine why anyone would call you that." Then he gave her a tiny goblet of nectar and said that he loved her and that when she knew him better perhaps they might marry and she would be his queen.

And Thumbelina thought of the toad and the stag beetle and the mole and the life she had left behind and smiled very sweetly at him and said that perhaps she would.

The Sleeping Beauty

In a land far away there once lived a king and queen who had everything they wanted in the world except a child. Every day they said longingly to each other: If only. . . . If only we had a child. But none was born to them.

Then one day in the early summer it happened that the queen was bathing in a clear pool close by the castle when a frog came swimming up through the water, climbed upon a lily pad as green as he was, and sat watching her. The queen spoke courteously to the frog and the frog croaked once or twice and puffed out his throat as frogs do when they have messages to deliver and said to her, "Madame, your wish has been fulfilled. Before a year has passed you shall bear a child." And without further remark he leaped into the pool and swam away.

Summer passed, fall came, and winter, and the trees lost their leaves. In the spring, just as the frog had prophesied, the queen bore a fine healthy daughter who squalled lustily and before she was even a month old smiled like an angel at her parents, who were as pleased as if they had made her themselves.

When a month had passed, the royal couple prepared a feast to celebrate the birth of their daughter. Along with the nobility and even the most humble folk of the kingdom they invited the fairies, for they knew how important it was that they be favorably disposed to the child. Indeed, they set out their twelve golden plates for the fairies to eat from. They had, unfortunately, forgotten a thirteenth fairy, a very old and hideous wizard who had not been seen for years. Some said he had gone up in a puff of smoke, others that he had been dissolved by one of his own poisons. In any case, it is doubtful the king and queen would have invited him, for they had only twelve golden plates. Perhaps they hoped that, even if he were alive, he would not hear of the feast.

But of course he did. The day of the feast came and each fairy in turn presented the child with a magic gift. One gave her good sense, one good luck, one generosity of spirit, one beauty, and so on until it seemed that little Briar Rose (for so she had been named) would have everything a princess could desire or need. Then, suddenly, just when the eleventh fairy had finished speaking, the floor of the banquet hall cracked open and up from the foundations and cellars of the castle came the thirteenth fairy, the old wizard, who prided himself on avenging the least slight to his dignity and position. He spoke to no one, not even to his colleagues among the fairies, but called out in a loud voice, "The princess shall prick herself with a spindle in her fifteenth year and fall down dead." And with that he disappeared into the crack and the floor closed up behind him.

For a moment everyone was struck dumb with horror. Then the queen picked up her baby from the cradle

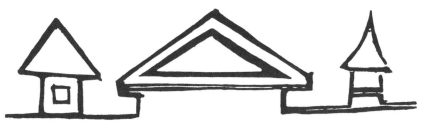

and began to weep. Just then the twelfth fairy, who
had not yet spoken, stepped forward.

"It is beyond my power to cancel this dreadful
curse," she said to the weeping mother, "but at least I
can soften it. Although your daughter will indeed fall
into a deathlike trance in her fifteenth year, my gift to
her is that she will not be dead but sleeping. She will
sleep a hundred years, until she is awakened by the
prince who is destined to find and love her."

The king, thinking to guard his daughter from so
terrible a fate, sent word through the kingdom that
every spindle and spinning wheel should be destroyed.
Henceforth the people would wear clothes of fur or
leather or felt. (Some, the poorest, were even reduced
to wearing clothes of leaves or bark.)

So the years passed and little Briar Rose grew tall
and lovely and kind and clever, and the king and
queen felt sure they had safeguarded her from the wizard's curse.

But one day in her fifteenth year, Briar Rose, wandering through the upper rooms of the castle, as she
often did, came to a little door she had never seen before and when she opened it and stepped in, she saw
an old woman with a spindle and a heap of flax at her
feet. How she came there, who can tell? But there she
sat, twirling the spindle and drawing out the thread.
Briar Rose, of course, had never seen such a thing in
her life and she was both puzzled and curious.

"Good day, then, Granny," she said. "What are you
doing here and what is that you have in your hand?"

"I am here because I am here," the old woman said.
"And as anyone can see, I am spinning."

"Spinning?" said Briar Rose. "And what is that
thing that twirls around in your hand? Is it a top?"

"Not exactly," said the old woman, "although something like. It is a spindle for making thread."

"May I try to spin, then?"

"Of course you may," said the old woman. "Why not?"

Briar Rose took the spindle and tried to twirl it, but she had scarcely touched it before she pricked her finger and in an instant fell into a deep sleep.

Below, the king, who was in the counting house with the royal treasurer, fell asleep over his gold. The queen dropped her snips and fell asleep in the rose garden, the horses went to sleep in the stable and the hens tucked their heads under their wings and slept on their nests. The fire on the hearth died and the pot stopped boiling. Even the cook, who was beating the scullion instead of the batter, sat down on his stool, leaned his head on his hand and dropped lightly off. On top of the henhouse the cock went to sleep in the middle of a crow and the fox who was watching him hungrily from a thicket, lay down as if he might never care to hunt again.

Around the castle a hedge of briar roses began to grow up. Every day it grew thicker and higher. The thorns were as sharp as needles and even the leaves had edges that cut like razor cane. No wind blew through the hedge—everything was still as death. Soon the castle itself was as invisible as if it had never been.

The years passed, and people spoke of the castle and the sleeping princess behind the thicket as if their very existence were a legend. From time to time princes who came to hunt in the forest nearby tried to force their way through the thicket. They brought their squires and men-at-arms with axes and flails to clear the way, but as quickly as the thicket was cut down it grew back twice as strong and dark and forbidding as before. It was said by some that hunters and even a prince or two had been caught by the thorns and that the briar bushes had grown around them and held them fast, so that they died miserably.

Many years passed in this way until at last the day came when a young prince from a neighboring kingdom chanced to be hunting in the forest near the rose hedge. When darkness fell, he sought shelter in the hut of an old man who lived at the edge of the forest, and as they sat talking over the fire, the old man told him the tale of the castle hidden behind the briar hedge and of the princess who, his grandfather had told him many years ago, must sleep a hundred years. He told also of the princes and hunters who used to come and try their strength and cunning against the briar hedge and how none had succeeded in piercing it and some had died.

Then the young prince determined to have a try. "I am not afraid," he said to the old man. "If this princess really sleeps there, I will find her and bring her out."

The old man tried to dissuade him with stories of a horrible death awaiting him, but the prince paid no attention, and next morning he set out toward the hedge.

As it happened, this was the very day the ancient curse pronounced by the old wizard would run its course. When the prince approached the briar hedge, instead of bristling and reaching out to pierce him with its thorns and sharp leaves, it began instead to flower. Briar roses with stamens as yellow as gold and petals the palest pink sprang open everywhere and the forest was filled with their fragrance. The prince advanced through the thicket with his sword drawn, but the branches bent aside and let him pass through unharmed.

When he came out into the paved courtyard of the

castle, the prince saw the queen sleeping in the rose garden and in the stable the horses dozing in their stalls and on the henhouse roof the rooster clinging to his perch. Still holding his sword at the ready, the prince entered the castle and saw there the courtiers asleep in the throne room and the king in the treasury. At first everything was so still his steps rang out on the stone like the clang of horses' hooves, but then a light breeze began to blow, and he heard the leaves of the trees whispering and speaking to each other outside the castle windows. Up and up through the castle he climbed, until at last he opened the door of the little tower room where Briar Rose lay sleeping, the spindle by her hand, a drop of blood trembling on her finger.

She was so lovely that the prince could scarcely believe his eyes. He lifted her in his arms and kissed her lips and then he kissed away the drop of blood on her finger and she opened her eyes and looked about her.

"I was learning to spin," she said. "Where is the old granny who was teaching me to spin?"

"As for that, who knows?" said the prince. "But

perhaps you would like to learn other skills, such as how to be a queen and rule a kingdom."

"As for that," said Briar Rose, "my mother and father have already taught me most of those skills, but. . . ." Then she broke off and looked at the prince, who was still holding her in his arms. "Put me down, please," she said, and the prince set her on her own two feet.

Downstairs the cook woke up and began to beat the batter instead of the scullion, the fox gathered his legs under him to spring, the rooster crowed and flapped up into the apple tree, and the king and queen and all the court awoke and went about their business. Even the pot began to boil and the flies to buzz at the window. Hand in hand the prince and Briar Rose made their way down from the tower and, after they had got better acquainted, the two fell so in love they knew they must never part. Their wedding was celebrated with great splendor, their two kingdoms were united, and they ruled happily and justly for the rest of their lives.

The Frog Prince

One summer afternoon a thousand years ago today, when the sun shone through the green leaves and made moving patterns on the stones, a princess played by the well in a palace courtyard and amused herself by tossing her golden ball into the air and watching the light flash from its surface as it fell. Higher and higher she tossed it, running here and there to catch it as it came down. But at last it flew too high and the light blinded her and she missed her catch and when it came down, it fell into the well.

Sitting on the coping and looking deep into the shadows of the well, the princess saw her face reflected in the circle of light on the water far below, but her golden ball had sunk to the bottom and there was no way she could retrieve it.

Then she began to lament and said aloud, "Alas, if only I could get back my golden ball, there is nothing I would not give—even my jewels or all my fine clothes or my golden crown."

Then an ugly brown-spotted green frog with a wide grinning mouth put its head out of the water and

63

croaked. "What is the matter, Princess?" said the frog. "You weep and lament so sadly that even as cold a creature as I must pity you."

"What business is it of yours, frog?" said the princess. "But if you must know, I have lost my golden ball that I love more than anything else in the world and I would give all that I own to get it back."

"I care nothing for your jewels and your golden crown, princess," said the frog, "but I will swim down and get your ball for you, if you will make me a promise."

Then the princess looked at the frog and thought perhaps it was true that he could retrieve her ball for her. "Anything! I will promise you anything, dear frog," she said, "only bring me back my ball."

"Let me sit by your side tonight at table," said the frog, "and eat from your golden plate. Let me sleep beside you on your little bed, and I will bring you your ball again."

The silly creature, the princess said to herself. What nonsense he talks. He cannot get out of the well, and if he could—if he tried to hop through the door of the palace—I would have the doorman squash him. So she said, "Certainly, dear frog. Bring me my ball and all shall be as you wish."

The frog swam deep into the well and brought up the golden ball and, leaning down, the princess took it from his mouth and sprang up and skipped away.

"Wait. Wait for me," said the frog. "Take me with you as you promised."

But the princess did not even look back.

That night, as all the court were going in to dinner, there was a knock at the palace door, and the princess herself, who had just run down the broad marble staircase, went and opened it.

There sat the frog, dripping with water and trailing ropes of treacle from the well.

She was so startled she slammed the door without a word and hurried in to the banquet hall to take her place at her father's right hand.

Then her father asked her what she was afraid of and who had knocked at the door. "For," he said, "you are as pale as if you had seen a dragon."

Then the princess shrugged and said in a low voice, "Oh, it's only a silly old frog who swam down into the well and brought back my ball to me this afternoon. I promised that he should come and sit by me and eat from my golden plate and sleep tonight in my bed, never thinking he could get out of the well. But there he is at the door, all dripping and slimy."

Even as she spoke, the frog knocked again and croaked in a loud voice.

The the king said, "As you have made a promise, my daughter, you must keep it. Go then and let the frog in and take him up beside you and let him eat from your plate."

So the princess let him in, but she could not bear to look at him and hurried back to the table and the frog hopped along behind her. "Take me up," he said, "that I may sit beside your plate." But she delayed until at last the king commanded her to do as she had promised. Then the frog ate with great pleasure from the princess's golden plate, but she, when she looked at him, could scarcely swallow a bite.

Afterwards the frog demanded that she take him up and carry him to her room and let him lie in her silken bed with a down pillow under his head. The princess wept, for she had heard from her old nurse that if she even touched such a creature, warts would come on her hands and body. And who could say what would happen if she let him lie down beside her?

But the king gave her a stern look. "How can you despise the creature who has helped you and to whom you have given your word?" he said.

So she took the frog by one leg and, holding him out at arm's length, carried him up to her room and dropped him on the floor in a corner. Then she turned the lamp low and lay uneasily down to sleep.

When she was in her bed, the frog hopped across the room and with a mighty leap hopped in beside her and put his head on her pillow and stretched himself out next to her.

But now the princess was alone, where no one could see what she did, and she snatched up the frog and threw him against the wall with all her strength. "There, you horrid creature," she said. "Let that show you what happens to frogs that aspire to sleep with princesses."

When he struck the wall, the frog's skin split and out stepped a prince, a king's son, the handsomest she had ever seen, and he told her how he had been bewitched by a wicked fairy, and how no one could deliver him from the well but a princess who would let him eat from her plate and sleep in her bed. Tomorrow, he said, they would go to his kingdom where he would make her his queen.

Then, the story goes, he lay down beside her, and she was so captivated by his beauty that she embraced and kissed him, and they made merry all night long.

And the next day, amid general rejoicing, they were wed (lest the christening follow too soon on the wedding). The princess's father blessed them and they mounted a golden coach and departed for the prince's kingdom where they lived happily until they died.

And the story goes, too, that when they drove away in their golden coach, drawn by six white horses, the prince's faithful servant Henry rode beside the coachman. Faithful Henry had been so grieved when his master had been changed into a frog that he had put three iron bands around his heart to keep it from breaking with grief. Now, as the carriage rolled down the highroad, the happy couple heard a cracking sound and the prince cried out, "Henry, the axle is breaking."

"No, master," said Henry. "It is not the axle. It is the band I forged round my heart when you were a frog and imprisoned in the well."

Again and once again while they were on their way, something cracked, and each time the prince thought it was the axle breaking. But it was the bands springing loose from the heart of faithful Henry because his master was set free and was happy.

So say some. But others wonder, and some say that it was poor Henry's heart bursting even the bands he had forged, at the thought of his master, bound for life to the treacherous princess who had broken her pledged word and thrown him against the wall.

The White Cat

There was once a king who had three sons, and like many another before him, he was of two minds regarding his kingdom and how he should dispose of it. One day he said to himself that he would reign until he died and let the sons quarrel among themselves and settle the succession however they chose, and another day he said to himself that he should put them to some test or other and see which was best fitted to rule. At last he made up his mind to put them to a test, and so he called them before him. "I have decided, my sons," he said, "that, old as I am, I should relinquish my crown to whoever among you is most resourceful. I plan to retire to my country estate and enjoy my old age in leisure. I would like to take with me to amuse me a little dog—the cleverest and most beautiful in the world. Your task, then is to go out into the world and find this creature for me. Whoever among you brings me the finest dog shall be king."

If the brothers thought this a curious way to decide the succession, they did not say so. Why should they,

since they had no choice in the matter? Instead, swearing eternal friendship to each other, they set out the next day on their quest, and came very shortly to a point where the road divided, two wide roads curving away to the south and the west and a third narrow trail leading eastward into a deep forest. Now the two older brothers thought to themselves that they were far more experienced and resourceful than the youngest and they were not concerned that he might find a dog finer than any they could find, so they thought only of how they could outdo each other. They each chose one of the wide roads leading to rich cities and great seaports. The youngest, deferring to his brothers, took the path into the forest. Then, agreeing to meet at this spot on the same day a year hence, the three parted. As the day advanced, the youngest made his way deeper and deeper into the woods. All was quiet. He passed no traveler and heard only the far-off musical calls of water thrushes and orioles and some-

times the sound of flowing water. When night fell he
wrapped himself in his cloak and lay down under a
tree to sleep. But shortly a storm came up. Rain fell in
sheets and drenched him to the skin, and he got up
and walked on, hoping to find shelter. He had not
gone far when he saw a bright light shining through
an opening in the trees and, making his way in that
direction, was amazed to see before him a magnificent
palace. The doors were of burnished gold set with
huge rubies and diamonds and emeralds, and on either
side torches in tall brazen standards cast a light that
flashed from the gems which flickered and shone like
blue and crimson flames. He pulled the heavy golden
ring in the middle of the door and heard within the
tinkling of a bell. Immediately the doors opened wide.
There was no one to be seen—only (floating in the air)
two pairs of hands which reached out and took him by
the arms and drew him in. He stood, amazed, gazing
about him at the richly furnished hallway until other

hands pushed him forward and guided him through marble corridors and into an apartment where clothes were laid out for him. Here the hands dressed him in a suit of brocaded velvet and brought a golden basin to wash his hands in and held a mirror so that he could comb his hair. Afterwards they guided him to a dining hall on the walls of which were hung portraits of all the famous cats of history—Puss in Boots, Dick Whittington's cat, sorcerers who had become cats, Robinson the musical cat—and also the cat ceremonies of witches' revels.

The table was set for two. The prince sat down and waited to see what would happen next. He had scarcely seated himself when an orchestra of cats dressed in evening clothes arranged themselves on a low dais and began to play and sing for him, some strumming guitars, others playing cornets and lutes, and some mewing together in four-part harmony. After the first song, the orchestra played a fanfare and a company of cat courtiers, some wearing swords and carrying plumed hats and others bearing rattraps full of rats and cages of mice, entered the hall led by a small figure only twenty inches high who was richly dressed and veiled from head to foot. When she stood before the prince, the little figure threw back her heavy veil and the prince saw the loveliest little white cat he had ever beheld. Her slanting green eyes were so sorrowful and her mew so sweet that his heart was touched.

"My lord," said the cat lady, "welcome to my palace."

The prince rose and made his hostess a deep bow. "Gracious lady," he said, "I see that you are no ordinary cat, but a powerful princess. Permit me to thank you for your kindness to me, a poor traveler who was ready to drown in the storm raging yonder in the forest."

"I am indeed mistress of all you see here," the little

cat replied, "but that is of no importance. What is important is that I am lonely and that you may divert me in my loneliness. But come, let the music continue and let us sit down to supper and conversation."

Hands brought in supper and served the two. There were two dishes, one of pheasants in the Hungarian style, the other of fat grilled mice. When the prince saw the mice, impaled on skewers, his appetite failed him, but the white cat assured him that his own dish had been prepared quite separately from hers; so, famished after his long day, he ate heartily. As he ate, he glanced from time to time at his hostess and observed that she wore on her front paw a bracelet of gold filigree framing a porcelain miniature. When he asked if he might examine it, she held out her paw willingly and he saw that the face painted on the porcelain bore a startling resemblance to him. But being a discreet young man, he asked no questions, saying to himself that when she was ready, she would tell him the history of the portrait. When supper was over, the cat princess with a wave of her paw called in a company of monkeys who performed a lovely ballet and then she directed the hands to show the prince to his chamber and bade him sleep well.

Next morning the prince awakened to the sound of hunting horns outside his window and, rising, found the attendant hands waiting to dress him in hunting attire. Outside, the princess awaited him, mounted on a monkey and clad in a red hunting jacket and bowler and accompanied by a great crowd of mounted cats and footmen holding greyhounds on the leash or winding their horns. The attendant hands mounted the prince on a wooden horse which, the princess explained to him, would gallop, when he wished, as fast as an Arabian courser. And when the prince inquired what their quarry might be, the princess said, "Mice, naturally, and perhaps rats, and a few rabbits," and set off at a gallop with all her troop.

When the day's sport was ended, they supped together again and the cat princess's conversation was so delightful that the prince forgot entirely the task his father had set him. In the days that followed there was no trouble to which his hostess would not go to amuse and divert him, and as time passed, he sometimes wished that he might be a cat and pass the rest of his life in her company. Almost a whole year went by, and still the prince did not set out on his quest. Finally one day the White Cat said to him, "Do you know there are only three days left for you to find the dog your father wants? Your two brothers have already found theirs and are on their way home."

Then the prince was thoroughly ashamed. "Alas," he said, "your company has charmed me so that I have forgotten everything in the world except you."

"Never mind," the little cat replied. "Do as I say and all will go well."

And on the appointed day, she first told him to mount the wooden horse on which he'd spent so many happy hours at the chase, and then she gave him an acorn. "Here is the dog," she said. "Put the acorn to your ear and you will hear him barking. Now go your way."

So the prince thanked her again and again for her kindness and told her how loath he was to leave her and mounted the horse and in a moment was transported to the crossroads where he had promised to meet his brothers. There they awaited him and the three rode on toward their father's palace, the two elder talking of their adventures and showing their dogs, which were so small and exquisitely fine that they seemed too fragile to handle. But our prince said nothing of the acorn he had in his pocket and suffered without remark his brothers' curious glances at his wooden horse. When they asked him if he had found a dog, he only nodded his head.

"Where is it, then?" said the eldest, but the prince

only smiled and his brothers concluded that he was simple-minded.

Next morning the three went in together to their father, who found the two little dogs, each one in its basket, so enchanting he could not make up his mind between them. Then our prince brought out his acorn and opened it. Inside a tiny black dog with hair as fine as spider's silk lay on a silken cushion. And when the prince set it on the table, it stood on its hind legs and danced like a circus dog and then bowed before the king and sat up and folded its tiny paws and begged. The king was amazed and said that the youngest son's dog was certainly the finest.

"But," said the king, "I am still in doubt which of you should be king and I feel that I am quite capable of ruling one more year. So I have decided to set you another task. Go out, therefore, and return in a year's time with the finest length of cloth you can find. I should like it to be at least fine enough to pass through the eye of a needle such as is used in lace-making."

This seemed an impossible task, but the brothers nevertheless set out as they had before. The two older ones were furious at the thought of this ridiculous quest, but the youngest mounted his wooden horse and trusted himself happily to the forest path. In a trice he was back at the palace of his beloved cat, who had languished and grown thin and pale with loneliness in his absence. When she saw him, she stretched her claws, arched her back and leaped straight up onto the mantelpiece out of sheer joy.

The prince told her of what his father now demanded and with a wave of her paw she replied that she would set her cats to spinning and weaving so that the cloth would be ready at the year's end. In the evening she ordered a great fireworks display to celebrate the prince's return and, at the prince's request, pardoned four miscreant cats who had been condemned to death for trafficking in stolen catnip.

Again the year passed in conversation and games and listening to sweet music. Sometimes the prince wondered about the portrait miniature on the White Cat's wrist, but still he kept discreetly silent. When the year ended, the cat princess again reminded him that he must return to his father's palace. This time she brought out for him a carriage of shining silver, all chased and engraved with waves and scallop shells and decorated on the doors with crests showing two Manx cats rampant. It was drawn by six matched gray horses and followed by a troop of men-at-arms.

"Go, my friend," she said to the prince, "and take with you this peach pit. In it you will find a piece of linen that will serve your purpose. Do not break it until you are in the presence of the king."

"Dear cat," said the prince, "pray let me stay here with you. I care nothing for my father's kingdom. Let my brothers quarrel over it, or let him keep it forever. Why should I deprive them of what they desire and I care less for every day?"

"King's son, you are kind to value so much the friendship of one like me who is good for very little except catching mice," said the White Cat, "but you must go where fate leads you. Set out then and do not tempt me to keep you here."

So the prince kissed the cat's paw and departed.

When he arrived at the palace, his brothers had come before him and had already laid out their linens, which were surely the finest and most beautiful ever seen in that kingdom, but they were not so fine that they could pass through the eye of a needle. The brothers had put on long faces and the courtiers and ladies murmured behind their hands that the king's demands were unreasonable, and some had even begun to speak out in the sons' behalf when all heard the sound of trumpets and our prince's carriage drew up at the palace gate and he alighted and came into the hall. He saluted his father and his brothers, produced the peach pit, and cracked it. Inside, instead of a piece of linen, he found a walnut. Then the people began to murmur and snicker at such foolishness and the brothers folded their arms and looked superior. Our prince took no notice, but cracked the walnut and found inside a hazelnut and inside that a cherry stone. Then the people laughed aloud and the prince himself doubted what he saw and murmured to himself, "What kind of trick is this you are playing, my sweet puss?" Instantly he felt an unseen paw scratch the back of his hand and a drop of blood welled up. "Ah, you are here beside me, I see," whispered the prince, and no longer doubting, he cracked the cherry stone. Inside he found a grain of wheat. Opening the wheat, he drew out a piece of linen a hundred yards long into which were woven scenes of cities and harbors, wheat fields, orchards, and village festivals, and the borders of which were decorated with intricate patterns of trailing vine tendrils, swimming fishes, and flying birds.

The king's face turned pale, for he was still of two minds as to the disposition of his kingdom and the fitness of his sons, and he had, indeed, decided that the joys of country life were not for him. Nevertheless, he had the needle brought and the web of linen slipped through the eye as easily as if it were a single silken thread. Then the king sighed and shook his head. "All the same," he said sternly, "I have the welfare of the kingdom at heart and it has crossed my mind that no king should rule without a queen (unless, of course, as in my case, the dear lady has passed away). Go, therefore and travel for one year longer and the one of you who brings the fairest bride, he shall be king."

The two older brothers accepted this additional task quite cheerfully and immediately set out, but although, as you know, our prince was a good-natured fellow, it occurred to him that since he had been twice successful, his father's injustice was directed solely against him. All the same, saying to himself that in his view there were cats in the world more charming than any human ladies, he entered his carriage and returned as he had come to his dear princess. He found her awaiting him in the throne room where the cat orchestra played a fanfare to greet him and the chorus mewed songs of welcome.

"We have been awaiting you," said the White Cat. "But how is it you return without the crown?"

"Dear lady," said the prince, "my father seems far more loath to give up his crown than I am eager to possess it. He has sent us forth again with another task."

"I know," said the cat, "and when the time comes we will deal with this new task. Meantime, however, I have been awaiting your return before beginning a battle—a naval engagement—which we must fight with the rats of this country, whose temerity grows daily. They infest our grain fields and storage bins and feast on our bounty. Indeed some of them are almost as large as I am and as fierce as wolves. . . . My cats fear water, it's true, but their size gives them in most cases an advantage that will equalize the contest." The prince and the cat princess walked out onto a terrace overlooking the sea where the battle was about to begin. The vessels of the cats floated high in the water, so that the sailors would not get their feet wet, and they were armed with rockets and roman candles and Catherine wheels to shoot at the rats. The rats, who were excellent swimmers, attacked from the shore, hurling landing nets over the deck railings, swimming or paddling out in their dinghies and scrambling nimbly up and over the side with their knives between their teeth. Together the prince and the cat princess directed the fleet now this way and now that. The battle was dreadful. A dozen times the rats were driven back, only to attack again, until at last Admiral Minagrobis, highest admiral of the cat fleet, reduced the rats to confusion by eating up their general. Then the white cat gave the signal to break off the battle. She had no wish to destroy the enemy completely, for, if there were no rats in the country, hunting would be dull (mice being much less challenging) and her diet monotonous.

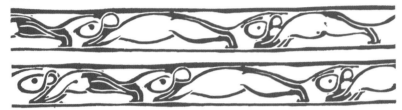

Another year passed in riding, hunting, playing chess, and other amusements. Now the prince sometimes begged his little friend to tell him the story of her life—for he was sure she must be under an enchantment, or else a fairy who preferred to live in the form of a cat, but she always turned aside his questions until at last toward the year's end, she reminded him that the time had come to return to his father's court. On this occasion she told him, too, that the time had come to put him to another test—a test on her behalf.

"You must kill me," she said.

The prince drew back in horror. "Never," he said. "Never would I harm the least hair of your little paw. For you are dearer to me than life. I care nothing for my father's kingdom. Only let me stay here always with you."

"You must kill me," the cat princess repeated sternly, and she had a sword brought, of finest Damascus steel, and laid on the table before him.

Again the prince shook his head. "Rather you kill me," he said.

"Steel yourself, my friend," she said, "and, if you

love me, do as I tell you. Take this sword and cut off my head and my tail and throw them into the fire. Your happiness and mine depend upon you. Take courage, then, and act."

Half-blinded by tears, the prince took up the sword and with one swift stroke cut off the cat princess's head. With another he severed her tail and threw them both in the fire. To his astonishment, the cat skin fell away from the poor little body and there arose before him a beautiful maiden with slanting green eyes, tapering fingers, and lovely long fair hair. By his act he had broken the enchantment in which the little cat was trapped. Then all the lords and ladies trooped in with catskins thrown over their shoulders and pressed forward to thank him and to pay court to their mistress.

When they had withdrawn, the princess sat down beside the prince and took his hand. "My friend," she said, "now at last I can speak and explain to you the mystery of my life. Since my birth I have been the prisoner of a band of wicked fairies who, while my mother was pregnant, trapped her by tempting her with magic fruits into agreeing to give me to them. My poor mother suffered dreadfully for her act, as my father had her thrown into prison when he discovered what she had done. But alas, even though she suffered, she had not such a fate as mine. The fairies kept me all through my childhood in an enchanted garden and when I was fourteen they betrothed me to Migonnet, the dwarf king, a horrible creature with an enormous head and a nose so long that several birds could perch on it. He had eagle claws for feet and his legs were gnarled like tree roots and when I saw him, I thought that I would die rather than be his bride. I resolved to make my escape from the enchanted garden and one day, when by chance my attendant left the gate ajar, I slipped out and set forth into the world. I had not gone far along the road when I saw an old woman sitting by the roadside weeping. I asked her what was the matter, and she said that she was weeping for my fate, as the fairies would soon overtake and recapture me and God alone knew how they would punish me for my disobedience.

"'Advise me, Granny,'" I said. "'What can I do to escape their wrath?'

"'There is no way to escape them, my dear', she said. 'For their chariots are swift and are drawn by winged dragons. But take this bracelet and wear it on your wrist always. When you meet the man whose portrait is painted thereon, he is the one who will release you from their spell.'

"She had scarcely finished speaking, handed me the bracelet, and disappeared into the shadows by the roadside, when the fairies swooped down on their fiery dragons and seized me. In their fury they turned me and all the lords and ladies of my father's kingdom into cats and brought me to this palace. Only some few they rendered invisible, all but their hands. It was from these that I learned the story of my birth and that my father and my poor mother were dead.

"So," said the princess, "I waited and mourned these seven years, looking every day at the portrait on my bracelet, and at last you appeared. Not only do you resemble the portrait, but you have proved willing to meet the final requirement—to cut off my head and tail and burn them. Now, dear prince, my misery is ended. Let us set out for your father's palace."

When they arrived, riding again in the Cat Princess's silver carriage, she hid herself in a lump of rock crystal, which the prince took up and carried into the throne room. There he found his two brothers, each with as beautiful a princess on his arm as anyone could dream of.

The king looked at his youngest son. "You come alone," he said.

"Your Majesty," replied the prince, "in this crystal you will find the loveliest little white cat in the world,

and indeed I love her more than ever I could love a princess."

Then the brothers and all the court laughed at such an absurdity and the king reached out to touch the crystal. At that moment the crystal sprang open and the cat princess, a queen now in her own right, stepped out in all her dazzling beauty, her hair as silver and gold as the moon and the sun and a garland of flowers girdling her white robe. At the sight the king, who was quite overcome, bowed down before her and said, "Beautiful lady, I cannot resist you. Be my son's wife and queen of this kingdom."

"Sire," she replied, "I have no wish to deprive you of your throne. Indeed, I have six kingdoms of my own. Allow me to offer one to each of your two elder sons. From you I ask only your blessing upon my marriage to your youngest son."

Then the king, who was delighted to continue to reign and said to himself that such must be the will of God, bowed gracefully and all the courtiers and their ladies cheered, and then and there the three marriages were celebrated with great pomp and rejoicing.

Beauty and the Beast

L ong ago in a city by the sea there lived a rich merchant who had three sons and three daughters. For many years he sent out his ships and traded for spices and gold and silks in far countries. But then he fell upon evil times. News came to him first that a storm in the Indian Ocean had sunk his ships, and then that the camel train bearing his spices from Arabia had been attacked by robbers and everyone of his servants killed save only the one who brought back the story. Still, he had gold in his strongboxes and he thought to remedy his losses, but fire broke out in his store room and all that he had was destroyed and his creditors came and claimed even the house where he and his children lived, so that they were forced to leave the city and travel to the small farm in the country where the merchant had spent his boyhood. Here they had nothing. The sons worked in the fields and the daughters, who had lost all their jewels and fine clothes and had no dowries, were left at home to mope and mourn their sad fate.

Now the two older girls indeed did nothing but sulk and complain; but the youngest, who was so fair that her father had always called her Beauty, wasted no time in weeping. Instead, she set about making the farmhouse clean and warm for her father and brothers when they came in from the fields. She washed and mended the work clothes and, when she had an idle hour, gathered the seeds of wildflowers in the hedgerows and woods nearby—trillium and wild hyacinths for the shade and black-eyed Susans and golden rod and maypops (which some call passion flowers) for the sunshine—and made a garden where in the summer evenings she sat and listened to the locusts singing and the cries of nightjars.

Thus some months had passed when one day a messenger came from the city saying that a ship which all had thought lost was come into port and that a part of the cargo was theirs. The two elder daughters dried their tears and began to talk of gold for their dowries and of jewels and fine linens. And the sons, too, talked of setting themselves up in business in the city. But Beauty, who said to herself that there's many a slip twixt cup and lip, said nothing, but went about, as she always did, preparing supper for the family.

Next morning the merchant, who had not so much as a donkey to ride, but only an ox for plowing, rose early to set out on foot for the city. Of each of his daughters he asked what he might bring back as a gift when he returned. The eldest asked for a jeweled tiara to wear in her hair and the second for a bolt of silk to make a ball gown, but Beauty felt a chill in the air and saw a cloud passing across the face of the sun and shivered with dread and said that all she wanted was her father's safe return. But he insisted, saying he would bring a gift whether she would or no and she should ask for what would please her. So she said, "Bring me a rose from the climber by the doorstep where we used to live, Father, for that was my favorite of all the roses in the world."

The merchant went on his way, but in the city he found that his treacherous partners had already divided the ship's cargo and left him nothing, and his creditors set upon him, clamoring for their gold and he was lucky not to end up in debtor's prison. So he turned toward home as he had come, a poor man.

Cold and hungry, he walked a long way until, when night fell, he was so weary that he thought he must lie down under the trees and make himself as comfortable as he could in a nest of fallen leaves. But just then snow began to fall and, as he looked about for a hollow tree or a cave to shelter himself, he saw a light far off. Thinking that it might come from the hut of a hunter or woodcutter who would give him food and lodging, he made his way in that direction.

He had walked only a little way when the woods opened out before him and he saw such a mansion—a palace indeed—as he had never seen before. When he took courage and knocked at the door, no one came, but the door opened slightly and he found himself in a lighted hall. He wandered through a dozen rooms, calling out now and then to make his presence known, but no one came. At last he found himself in a small apartment where soft music came from invisible harps and horns. There he saw a table with a chair drawn up to it and food and wine laid out, and in the fireplace a small fire crackled.

He said to himself that since no one was at home, surely the owners would not be offended if a cold and hungry traveler sat down there to his supper. So he ate and drank and listened to the music, and later he lay down in a bed in the next room and slept soundly. The next morning he rose, and still he saw no one. But a pitcher of water and a bowl had been set by his bed, and he washed and sat down again to breakfast before the fire. Then he resolved to set out for home and bring the news of his ruin to his children. Outside, the snow had vanished. A garden lay spread out before the palace with birds flying and roses blooming. At least, he said to himself, if I can bring nothing home to my other children, I can bring Beauty her rose. And he wandered through the garden until, seeing a climber just like the one by the doorstep of their old home, he drew his knife and cut one perfect blossom.

Then a roar sounded that shook the limbs of the oak trees and raised dust in the flower beds and, turning, he saw a Beast—a creature with hairy face and wide gleaming eyes and powerful shoulders all covered with coarse hair—tramping toward him through the garden. His tread was so heavy the ground shivered and the merchant shivered, too, and thought that he would faint with terror.

When the Beast stood before him, he lowered his shaggy head and roared again and snatched the rose from the merchant with a clawed hand. "Ungrateful man," he said, "I have taken you in when you might have died of cold and hunger in the forest. I have sheltered and fed you, and you. . . ! You return my kindness by stealing the most beautiful rose in my garden. Make your peace with God, then, for I intend to kill you."

Then the merchant fell on his knees and pled for his life, saying *My Lord,* and *God save your lordship* and the like, telling the beast all that had happened to him and saying at last that he had thought only to take one rose to his youngest daughter Beauty, who has asked for nothing more.

Then the Beast said, "Your flattery sits ill with me, merchant. My name is not *My Lord* or *Highness,* but Beast. All the same I pity you and your children, who

have suffered these misfortunes. I will forgive you then and free you to return to them and give you gold and jewels enough to please them and a rose for Beauty. All this, if you make me one promise.

Still on his knees, the merchant promised that he would do anything the Beast required of him and the Beast said, "My condition, then, is that you will return in a month's time and bring with you one of your daughters who will stay in your place. One of your daughters, who—listen well!—*must come willingly.*"

Now the merchant had not the least intention of sacrificing one of his daughters to save his own life, but he said to himself that he would take the gold and jewels to his children and return alone in a month's time. That way, at least he would leave his daughters with dowries and his sons with the means to set themselves up in the world. So he agreed, and the Beast, fulfilling his pledge, brought a coffer of gold and set the merchant on a swift white horse and filled his saddlebags with jewels and gave him the rose and sent him on his way.

In an eye's blink he was transported to the door of his cottage. There his children gathered around him and he told them of all that had befallen him, leaving out only that the Beast had said he must return in a month's time and bring with him one of his daughters, who must have consented willingly to take her father's place.

But when he looked on Beauty and gave her the rose he had cut in the Beast's garden, he could not help himself. "Alas," he said and burst into tears.

Then Beauty coaxed from him the whole story and, while her sisters drew back in horror, she said, "Console yourself, Father. When the time comes I will go with you."

Afterwards all the children and the father, too, put the matter from their minds, for indeed it was too terrible to think about. Instead they spent the month setting the brothers up in business and preparing dowries for the daughters. Only on the last day Beauty said to her sisters that they must divide her dowry between them, for she would go with her father.

Then the brothers said they would attack the Beast's castle and kill him and free their father from his promise. But the father shook his head and said that the Beast's magic was too strong for them and that, besides, he had given his promise. Either he would return alone or he would bring his daughter with him.

The two older sisters pretended not to hear his words and spoke about other matters and told how the young men in the neighborhood were already seeking their hands in marriage. But Beauty sat quietly by the fireside and looked out into her garden and said nothing.

Next morning, when she heard her father stirring, she rose and dressed and went to him and, when he drew back and said, "No!" she said, "Yes!" and she mounted the Beast's white horse behind him and in a moment they were transported to the palace where they found all as her father had described it.

Then Beauty, so as not to distress her father, put on a brave face and said that perhaps this beast was not so bad and would not require them to fulfill the pledge. Just then the Beast appeared and when Beauty saw him, she could not help shrinking back.

He saw and gazed at her with his great sad eyes under their shaggy brows, but all he said was: "So. You have come," to the merchant. Then he took the two of them to the banquet hall and had a feast set before them and left them to their last evening together.

Next morning at the palace door the Beast's white horse, his saddle bags loaded with gold and jewels, pawed the ground and snorted. The merchant mounted, his head bowed down with grief, and was borne away.

Then Beauty, fearing for her life, fell to weeping. But it was not in her to weep for long, and after a while she took courage and looked about her and began to explore the palace. She came soon to a rich apartment where everything was arranged for her comfort—books laid out on the tables, dresses hanging in the press, and fine stockings and lace-trimmed mantles in the cabinets. On the wall of the bedroom hung a sampler embroidered in gold with the words, "Beauty's Apartment."

Then she took heart, for it seemed to her as if the beast must be planning to keep her alive, since he had gone to so much trouble for her.

Still she was sad and, as she wandered through her rooms, she said aloud, "Alas, if only I could see my poor father and know that he has found his way safely home." Then, to her astonishment, a scene appeared in the mirror hanging on the near wall, and she saw her father dismounting from the Beast's white horse and greeting her sisters, who appeared to be more interested in the contents of his saddlebags than in him.

The day passed for Beauty in reading and listening to sweet music and, when night fell, invisible hands brought her dinner. As she sat down to the table, she heard the Beast's heavy step in the hall and he came and stood in the doorway and looked at her.

Beauty trembled when she saw him, but she tried to compose herself and greeted him courteously. "Hello, Beast," she said. "Welcome to my rooms. I give you thanks for all you have arranged for me."

Then the Beast, who still stood in the doorway, asked if he might come in and sit down.

"That's as you please," she said, "for this is your palace and I am your hostage."

But the Beast replied, "No, dear Beauty, you are mistress here and if you bid me be gone, I will go."

Beauty looked into his sad eyes and said nothing, and the Beast came in and sat down.

"Tell me," he said, "do you find me ugly? Is my presence so fearful that you would have me go?"

Beauty said, "I cannot lie to you, Beast. You are indeed ugly. But you have been so kind to my father and me that I know you must be very good-natured."

"It's true I have a kind heart," said the Beast, "but it's also true that I am not only hideous, but I lack understanding and am at best a stupid creature."

"Perhaps," said Beauty, "but when I hear you speak thus, it makes me think you lack vanity and it seems to me that humility is better than wit. Do sit beside me and keep me company while I eat."

Then they sat talking a long time, until at last the Beast rose to retire. He held out his hairy paw as if to take her hand and said, "Beauty, will you be my wife?"

Beauty could not conceal her horror, and she shrank back trembling, for surely, she said to herself, he will be angry at my answer. But she said only, "No, Beast, I cannot be your wife."

And at that he said in a mournful voice, "Farewell, then, Beauty," and left the apartment.

Alas, said Beauty to herself, how sad that any creature so kind should be so hideous.

Thus Beauty lived for many months. Every day she amused herself in her apartments and wandered through the palace gardens, and every night the Beast came and sat beside her. She found his company so pleasant that she would have looked forward to seeing him without a qualm except that every night he put to her the same question: Will you be my wife? and it made her sad every night to say, No.

Finally one night she said to him, "Beast, it distresses me to refuse you thus again and again, for I have come to care a great deal for you. But I cannot marry you."

"Don't distress yourself, Beauty," the Beast said. "I will not give up the hope that one day you will consent to be my wife. But meanwhile it would ease my heart if you would promise to stay with me forever, even if you cannot marry me."

Then Beauty, who every day watched her father and her brothers and sisters in the Beast's magic mirror, said, "Alas, Beast, perhaps I could consent to stay with you always, if only. . . ."

"If only what?" said the Beast. "Tell me."

"My poor father is alone now," said Beauty, "since my sisters are married and my brothers attending to their affairs in the city. It seems to me he grows thinner and I know he weeps when he thinks of my fate. If only I could visit him, perhaps I could consent to stay with you always."

The Beast sighed.

"Let me go for one week only," Beauty said. "I promise I will return to you."

So the Beast gave his consent, saying, "Go then, dear Beauty, but if you don't return to me as you promise in a week's time, I know I shall die of grief."

So again Beauty promised and the Beast gave her a ring and told her to lay it on the table beside her bed and when she wished to return to put it on and turn it around and say, "Return me to my Beast," and she would instantly be back in her own apartment in his palace. Then he gave her coffers of gold to take to her father and silks for her sisters and put her on his white horse and sent her on her way.

When Beauty's father saw her, how she was alive and unharmed, he was filled with joy and sent messengers to her sisters telling of her arrival and her good fortune, and the two sisters, who had used their dowries to find rich husbands, came for a visit.

They were wild with envy when Beauty told them of her life, for even though they were wealthy, they were not content. One's husband, she said, was handsome but so vain and stupid that he spent his days admiring himself and paid no attention to her, and the other said that hers was clever enough, as well as rich, but used his wit to torment her and make sport of her.

Why should Beauty be happy? they asked each other. Why should she live in a palace in the company of a kind beast when their lives were so miserable? In their jealousy, they plotted together to delay her return. "We will be so kind to her that she cannot bear to leave us," said the elder. "Yes, and we will tell her that if she goes, our father will die of grief," said the younger. "Then when she fails to go back on the appointed day, the Beast, whose magic is so powerful, will undoubtedly have her slain, or at least chained up in a vile prison, and it will serve her right."

So they wept whenever she mentioned leaving and sat with her in her garden and told her how they had missed her. Beauty listened to their treacherous words and delayed leaving from day to day. And so the week passed and another day and another. But on the ninth night she dreamed that she was in the palace garden and saw there her Beast lying under her favorite climbing rose. His poor face was pale under its hairiness and his eyes sunken, and he looked as if he might be dying.

Beauty sat straight up in bed and burst into tears.

"Oh, why did I leave him?" she cried. "My good Beast. By my treachery I have destroyed him." And she seized the ring from the table by her bed and put it on and turned it, saying, "Transport me to my Beast." In a moment she was in the garden, and there lay the poor Beast, just as she had seen him in her dream, holding a rose in his paw and lying as if dead under her rose bush.

She threw herself down beside him and took his poor head in her lap. "Oh, Beast," she said, "forgive me. I should never have left you." And feeling that his heart was still beating, she fetched wine from the palace and held his head so that he could sip a little, and the Beast opened his eyes.

"Dear Beast," Beauty said, "you must not die, but live and be my husband. In my blindness and foolishness I have almost lost you who are more precious to me than anyone in the world." And she stroked his rough hair and said again, "Live, and be my husband."

Then, all through the palace, music sounded, and in the garden all the trees bloomed, and lights shone everywhere and, when Beauty looked again at the Beast, he had vanished from under her hand. In his place, standing before her, was the handsomest young man she had ever seen. He bowed low to her and thanked her for having released him from the spell cast on him by a wicked wizard who had decreed that he must keep the shape of a beast until some maiden loved him enough to marry him in spite of his hideous appearance.

Then, with a wave of his hand, the prince brought into the palace garden Beauty's father and her three brothers and her sisters, and all rejoiced to see her, except the sisters, whose faces were still screwed up with spite and envy. Then the pair were married with great pomp and ceremony, and afterwards the prince brought Beauty's father to live with them in the palace. As for the sisters, it is said that, although the prince thought they should be turned into stones, Beauty, who was more generous-hearted than they had any right to expect, sent them back to live with their husbands in wealth and misery.

Puss in Boots

A certain miller, it is said, an old man who had come to the time of life when the accounts are balanced, called to his bedside his two sons. "I have been sent for to pay the debt we all owe nature," said the miller "and believe me, my sons, I would be happy to leave this world of trouble, but for the thought that I leave you without a coat to your backs. Even my mill is mortgaged to the money lenders. I am not worth so much as a fly would carry tied to its foot, for I have been dogged all my life by ill luck. Indeed, look at me. I am so ragged and tattered that if I could get out of bed, I would be naked as a flea. Nevertheless, I wish to leave you something at my death as a token of my love. Therefore, you, my first born, take the sieve hanging on the wall, with which you may, perhaps, sift out your living. And you," he said to the younger, "take the cat curled up there by the hearth, and may both of you remember your father and bless his name."

Having said this, he said, "Adieu. Darkness falls," and then he died.

Now after the two had laid him out and buried him, the elder took the sieve and went about sifting to gain a living and the more he sifted the more he gained. And the younger looked at the cat, who, being an excellent mouser, was considerably plumper than his master, and said in disgust, "Whoever heard of such an inheritance? I have nothing to eat for myself and now I will have to think for two. Better if he had left me nothing."

But the cat, hearing this, said to him with a grave and serious air, "Do not afflict yourself, master. But give me a bag and get me a pair of boots made that I may make an appearance worthy of you, and you shall see that I am not so bad an inheritance as you think."

The young man thanked the cat and gave him a pat on the back, although he put no faith in his words,

and seeing that he had no better course to follow, had the boots made and put himself in the cat's charge.

Next morning, when the sun began to gild the very stones in the roadway and turn the river to silver, the cat put on his boots, took his bag, and made his way to the riverside. Watching for his chance, he caught a carp as red as the sunrise and, putting it in his bag, made his way to the castle of the king of that country, where he asked to speak to his majesty. When he was shown into the king's apartment, making him a low bow, the cat said, "My lord, the Marquis of Carabas, a slave of your highness and a loyal subject, sends this fish with his humble greetings."

The king, with a kindly smile such as one generally wears to those who bring gifts, answered, "Say to this lord, whom I do not know, that I thank him."

Next day Master Puss booted himself and went into a part of the wood where he knew there were a great number of rabbits. There he put some lettuce leaves and bran and a carrot or two in a bag and, lying down, stretched out as if he were dead (although holding the strings of the bag between his paws) and waited. Scarcely had he settled himself when a pair of innocent young rabbits sniffed the food and went into the bag. Puss, pulling the cords tight, caught and killed the two and, going to the palace, announced himself as before and was ushered into the throne room, where he bowed low and said to the king, "Sire, I bring a pair of plump young rabbits from the warren of the Marquis of Carabas, which I am bidden to present to you on his behalf."

"Tell your master that I thank him and am gratified by his attention," said the king, and he ordered that gold coins be given to the cat and said to him again, "My deepest thanks."

Another time, the cat hid among the stubble of a corn field, keeping the mouth of his bag open. Two quail ventured in and, jerking the cords tight, he captured them both and took them to the king.

Thus the cat continued to prepare the way for his master for a fortnight or longer, and one day, when he knew for certain that the king would drive out by the river with his daughter, the most beautiful princess in the world, he said to his master, "If you will follow my advice, your fortune is made. You have nothing to do but go and bathe in the river just at the curve by the high road and leave the rest to me."

Then, after the miller's son had taken off his clothes and was bathing in the river, Puss, seeing the king's carriage approach, hid the clothes under a stone and began to call out, "Help, help. Stop, thieves."

At these shouts, the king ordered his carriage stopped and, looking out, saw the cat who had brought him so many gifts.

"Come to the aid of the Marquis of Carabas," shouted Puss and he ran up to the carriage window and explained to the king that while his master was bathing, robbers had come and stolen his clothes. At once the king offered his own cloak to cover the naked marquis and, taking him back to the palace, commanded the keeper of his wardrobe to bring a suit of his finest clothes for the marquis to wear.

As these set off the young man's good looks (for he had been handsome enough to begin with, and had grown fatter and stronger over the past month eating and drinking with the money which the king had given to Puss), the princess found him very much to her liking.

After the two young people had eaten and spent the evening talking and flirting and drinking the king's wine, they each begged leave to retire and were escorted to their separate chambers where the princess dreamed that perhaps she might marry this fine marquis, and the miller's son that he might be a prince and some day a king.

But the cat remained with the king and spent a long time telling him of the prowess and judgment of his master, not to mention his riches—which Puss said were so great that no account could be kept of them.

Next day the king sent for his trustiest counselors and bade them inquire regarding the Marquis of Carabas, and Puss, having foreseen that this might happen, ran on ahead of the officers and when he passed a meadow where workers were mowing, called out to them, "Ho, there, peasants, keep your brains clear. A company of robbers disguised as officers of the king is laying waste the countryside. If you wish to save your homes and your belongings, when they come near, you should say that all this land belongs to the estate of the Marquis of Carabas. Then no harm will befall you."

And so he continued to do all along the road, so that wherever the king's messengers arrived they heard the same song, telling of the riches of this lord.

At last Puss came to a stately castle, the master of which was an ogre, the richest in the land—for all the lands which the king's officers had passed belonged to him. The cat, who had taken care to inform himself regarding this ogre's skills, asked to speak with him and pay his respects. The ogre received him and bade him sit down.

"Rumor has come to me," said the cat, "that if you have a mind to, you are able to change yourself into all sorts of creatures."

"That's true," said the ogre, smoothing down his whiskers and examining himself in a mirror—for he was quite vain of his gifts. (And, as at that moment he was not hungry, he had decided to put off devouring the cat). "Let me convince you," said the ogre. And without another word he crouched on his throne and changed himself into a lion.

Puss was so terrified at this that he ran up the brocaded wall hanging (This he accomplished with great difficulty, on account of his boots) and perched on the throne room balcony.

The ogre gave a roar and resumed his natural shape—which was quite as frightening as his lion shape.

Then Puss leaped down from the balcony and, bowing deeply, went on. "I have also heard it said that you have the power to take on the shape of the smallest of animals—for example, a rat or a mouse. But I own that I don't believe this to be possible."

"Not possible!" The ogre ground his teeth and threw aside his mirror. "You shall see," he said, and he changed himself into a mouse and ran across the throne room floor to Puss's feet. "See," he squeaked, "What do you think of me now?"

Puss did not reply. Catching the ogre between his two front paws, he gave him a cuff and ate him up.

Meanwhile, the officers of the king had gone back to report their observations to their master and now the king himself with all his retinue had come out to see the lands of the Marquis of Carabas. As the procession approached the ogre's castle, Puss ran out into the roadway and called to the king, "Welcome, Your Majesty, to the castle of my lord Marquis of Carabas." Having seen all this wealth, the king took Puss up in his carriage and on the way back to the palace promised a reward to the cat if he would bring about a marriage between the marquis and his daughter. And the cat, pretending to go and come backwards and forwards, concluded the match, and the miller's son and the princess were married.

After a month

of high festivities, the new marquis took his bride home to his castle, and there he took over the management of the ogre's land. Finding himself in so fortunate a situation—happily married, and the possessor of a fine estate—the marquis took the cat aside privately and thanked him, saying that more good had been wrought for him by the craft of a cat than by the wit of this father. Therefore, he said, Puss could live with him always in luxury and never lift a paw. And he swore that when Puss died he would be embalmed with sweet unguents and spices and buried in a golden jar which he, the marquis, would keep in his room always.

Puss, upon hearing this vow, thought he would put the marquis to the test and a few days afterwards, pretending to be dead, stretched out on the hearth rug, rolled his eyes back and let his jaw drop open. Then the princess, seeing him, began to weep and called her husband, saying, "Oh, a terrible misfortune. I can scarcely bear to tell you."

"What is it?" cried the marquis. "Are the crops ruined? Is the castle on fire?"

"No, worse than that," said the princess. "Your beloved cat is dead."

Then the marquis replied, "Better him than ourselves. Let him take with him every evil that might befall us."

"What shall we do with him?" said the wife.

And the marquis said, "Take hold of a leg and throw him out the window."

Upon this, Puss leaped up in a fury. "Are these the thanks I get for ridding you of rags?" he said. "Is this the reward for my cunning? Scoundrel! Villain! God protect me from such a scoundrel. And as for that," he said to the wife, "God protect you from your husband when he no longer has need of you." And he took to his heels and went his way with boots and bag, resolved to use them for himself alone.

So say some. But others say that this account of the
end of the friendship between Puss and the miller's son
is a slander and that in truth the marquis kept his word
and always had a silk cushion by his chair, where Puss
rested in peace and comfort and never more hunted
either fish or rabbits or quail or mice except for his
own diversion.

Cinderella

Once upon a time there lived a wealthy merchant, a widower who had one daughter. As often happens, after a suitable period of mourning for his dead wife, he began to long for the companionship of a woman, and decided, therefore, to marry again, a woman who had lost her husband and had two daughters of her own. Now, whatever the reason, this woman was proud and haughty and able to think only of the welfare of her own daughters and to envy her husband's daughter, who, it is true, was a lovely and gentle young girl and promised to be a great beauty.

At first the new wife had only kind words for her stepdaughter and seated her above her own daughters at table and gave her the choicest of everything. But before long, when it was clear that the merchant was quite silly and doting with love for his new wife, she began by little and little to bring forward her own daughters and, as for her stepdaughter, by little and little the proud woman moved her from the head of the table to the foot, from the dais to the scullery, from the garden to the kitchen, and dressed her in coarse rags instead of fine silks. Her hair was greasy and tangled from the smoky kitchen air, her smock grew ragged, the soles of her shoes were worn, and her two stepsisters took to calling her Cinderella, saying that she looked as if she lived in the fire place.

Cinderella, all this time, scarcely noticing what was happening to her, was grieving for her dead mother. Every day she would visit her mother's grave and leave on it bouquets of black-eyed Susans and blue-eyed grass and sunflowers and maypops that she gathered by the roadside on her way to the churchyard. One day, as she walked toward the church, she made the acquaintance of an elderly lady, and afterwards this lady sometimes stopped her in the road to inquire after her welfare, and sometimes, since the lady seemed so kind and interested, the young girl would divide her bouquet of flowers and share them with her new friend—who was indeed the only person with a kind word for her.

Now, as happened from time to time in that kingdom, one day an invitation went out from the king to all the families round about to attend a great festival in honor of the king's beloved son. When Cinderella's family received their invitation, the stepmother and her daughters began to make their plans. There was to be a ball each night of the three days of the festival and the two girls said that they would be the most beautiful young ladies there. Naturally they would catch the prince's eye and perhaps he . . . Well, who could guess what might happen?

Cinderella, who was as light of foot as a fairy and who loved above all things to dance to the sweet music of the clavichord and the viola da gamba, listened to their talk and forgot for a while her grief for her dead mother. She longed to go to the ball—if only to dance one single dance.

"Please," she said to her stepmother one day as she listened to the talk of fine dresses and new silk stockings, "Please, may I go with you to the ball?"

The older sister laughed until she could scarcely catch her breath and the younger looked Cinderella up and down in her ragged smock and torn stockings, and then the two looked at each other and at their mother who barely glanced at Cinderella before she said, "Don't be ridiculous. How could anyone so dirty and ugly as you go to the king's ball?"

"Here, make yourself useful," said the older sister rudely, "hold this mirror while I try on my silver snood."

And the younger said, "Bring the iron and press my lace collar."

So Cinderella did as they bid with as much good nature as she could muster and then again asked if she might not go. "I could wear the yellow dress you wore for May Day," she said to the older sister, "if I took the waist in a bit."

"A cinder clod like you? What nonsense?" said her stepmother. And so they departed, holding their heads quite high and stiff so as not to muss their hair, and walking with great pain because their new shoes were too small.

When they were gone, Cinderella sat down by the hearth and wept.

At that very moment the old lady whom Cinderella had seen so often by the roadside must have been passing by. Or perhaps she had her own way of finding out what was happening in the world. In any case, when Cinderella looked up, there she was—standing in the open doorway. "Why are you weeping, Cinderella?" she asked.

"I should like . . . I should like . . ." Cinderella gave a great sob.

"You'd like to go to the ball, my dear?"

"Yes," said Cinderella. "But . . . But look at me. It's impossible."

"Oh, I don't know," said the lady. "Perhaps, after all. . . ." (For, in truth, she was Cinderella's fairy godmother who, all these months, had been keeping an eye on her and considering how she might help her.) "Things may not be so impossible as they seem," she said. "Let's see. Go into the garden and bring me a pumpkin."

When Cinderella brought the pumpkin, her godmother set it down by the front doorstep, scooped out the seeds, and touched it with her staff. Instantly the pumpkin was changed into a glittering golden coach. "What good is a coach without horses?" said the old lady. "Bring me from the kitchen that cage trap, which I doubt not has a few live mice in it," and when Cinderella brought the cage and set it down by the coach, a touch of her staff changed the mice into a matched team of prancing horses with coats of shining mousey-gray. "Now, let's see. Next, we must have coachmen."

"Ah, Godmother," said Cinderella, who was quite excited by now, "under the horse trough live a pair of green and yellow-spotted frogs. Perhaps. . . ."

"The very thing," said her godmother.

Cinderella ran to the horse trough and brought back the frogs, and in a moment they were handsome coachmen in green and yellow-spotted livery.

"Now, my dear," said the godmother. "Now for you." And she waved her staff three times. In a moment Cinderella stood before her, dressed in a ball gown that shone like silver, and on her feet were lovely slippers of spun glass.

As she entered the coach her godmother held up the staff. "One thing you must remember, my dear," she said. "Leave the ball before the clock strikes midnight, for although my magic is strong it lasts only until then."

Cinderella gave her promise and waved her hand and the coachman cracked his whip and away they whirled.

When the king's son heard of the arrival at the palace of a mysterious unknown princess, he led her into the ball room and claimed the first dance, and as they whirled round the floor to the music everyone gasped with astonishment at the beauty and grace of this unknown lady. Then the king's son led her into the banquet hall and seated her in the place of honor on his right and all evening had eyes only for her. And Cinderella's two stepsisters put on such sour faces that their mother pinched them black and blue and whispered to them that if they did not smile, they would never catch the prince's eye.

While all the company were still feasting, Cinderella heard the tower clock strike a quarter to twelve and rising from the table curtseyed deeply first to the king and then to his son and, with steps as quick and light as if she were flying, ran through the palace halls and out the front door, stepped into her coach and was whirled away into the night. At home, she found her godmother waiting and embraced and kissed her joyfully. "Tomorrow night you must go again, my dear," said her godmother. "But for now, back to your cinders."

When the stepsisters arrived, Cinderella was dressed as usual in her shabby smock and seated by the fireplace.

"Oh," said the elder, "you should have seen the strange princess who arrived late at the ball. The prince had eyes only for her and paid no attention to us, although surely our gowns were more beautiful than hers."

"He acted quite silly," said the younger.

"Rude!" said the elder.

"You must wear your green and purple dresses tomorrow night," said their mother, "and for goodness' sake, smile when he looks in your direction. It's no wonder he never danced with you. Your faces looked like dried prunes."

"What are you laughing at, Cinderella?" said the elder. "Stop acting the fool and help me with my stays. But wash your grubby hands before you touch me."

The next night the two sisters went to the ball—and so did Cinderella, and the king's son still had eyes only for her. But the third night Cinderella, who thought that she would like never to stop dancing, forgot her godmother's warning. The tower clock was sounding the sixth stroke of midnight when she fled from the prince's arms away through the palace corridors and down the steep palace steps. The prince ran after her, but he could not catch her. She and her coach vanished into the shadows and she left behind nothing except one of her glass slippers, which in her haste she had lost. When she reached home, all her finery had vanished and it seemed to her that she must have been dreaming.

But the next day she was awakened by the sound of trumpets, for the prince had sent out messengers through all the kingdom to proclaim that he would wed the princess to whom the glass slipper belonged. All the unmarried ladies of the kingdom—princesses, duchesses and dames—tried it on, but of course it fit none of them. And then the prince ordered his equerries to try it on every maiden in the kingdom, even the lowliest.

When they came to the house where Cinderella lived, the courtiers tried the slipper on each of the two stepsisters, who scrunched down their toes and struggled in vain to squeeze in their big feet. No one paid any attention to Cinderella, who sat by the hearth shelling peas, and the courtiers were preparing to go when she said quietly, "But I am here, too. Let me try the slipper."

The stepsisters were furious.

"She's only the kitchen maid," said one.

The other said, "Out, silly creature! Go slop the pigs," and even threatened her with the broom.

But Cinderella stood her ground and, as the equerries had been ordered to try the slipper on every maiden in the kingdom, one knelt and Cinderella put out her slender white foot, and the slipper fit as easily as if it were made for her, which of course it was.

Then she brought out the other slipper which she had concealed in her pocket and, when they saw that she had the mate, they bowed down before her.

At that moment Cinderella's godmother appeared and with a touch of her staff swept away the dust and cinders from her face and transformed her rags into a dress of rich blue velvet. Then all could see that she was indeed the mysterious princess with whom the prince had fallen in love.

The equerries took her up into the carriage and whirled her away to the palace where within a few days she was married to the young prince amid general rejoicing.

As punishment for their vanity and heartlessness, the godmother turned the two stepsisters into stone statues which she placed on either side of the palace gate. "Stay there," she said, "until your characters and dispositions have been improved by observing the behavior of your sister."

Some say that Cinderella interceded in their behalf and that at last her godmother relented and allowed them to be married to gentlemen in suitable circumstances.

As for the father, whose weakness in my view was the cause of Cinderella's misery, perhaps his punishment was to have to live the rest of his life with her wicked stepmother.

The Three Billy Goats Gruff

Once there were three billy goat brothers whose name was Gruff. In the winter their home was in a valley where they fed on hay and lived quite comfortably in a large barn. Every year when spring came they went up to the high mountain pastures where the grass was rich and green and the air cool and pleasant. To get there they had to cross a bridge over a swift mountain stream and one year it happened that just before they set out a troll moved in under the bridge—a great ugly troll with eyes as round and big as dinner plates and horns like a ram's and a nose as long as a sausage.

The youngest and littlest of the goats set out first from his fenced field through a deep wood of oak and pine trees until he came to the bridge where, as his brothers had warned him, the troll now lived. When he came to the bridge, he hesitated a minute and then over he went. *Trip, trap, trip, trap,* like drumsticks on a drum, his little hoofs beat a tatoo on the bridge.

"Ho, ho. Who is that tripping over my bridge?" called the troll in a voice as deep and croaky as a bull frog's.

"Oh, it's only me, the littlest Billy Goat Gruff," said the little goat, "and I'm going up to the high mountain pasture to eat the grass and make myself fat."

"Well, here I come to gobble you up," roared the troll.

"Oh, no, please don't eat me," said the little goat, tripping along as fast as he could. "Wait a bit for my brother, the second Billy Goat Gruff. He's coming along behind me, and he's much bigger and fatter than I am."

"Well, well," croaked the troll, grumpily. "Be off with you then, and don't bother me any more."

After a little while came the second Billy Goat Gruff, through the woods and then, *Trip, Trap, Trip Trap,* over the bridge.

"Who's that tripping over my bridge?" roared the troll in an even louder croak.

"Oh, it's only me, the second Billy Goat Gruff, and I'm going up to the pasture on the mountainside to eat the tender green grass and make myself fat. Don't let me disturb you," he added. "I'll be off the bridge in a moment."

"Not before I come and gobble you up," roared the troll, and he began to puff himself up and make himself as ugly and fierce as he could.

"No, no, no, you don't want me," said the second Billy Goat Gruff. "I'm stringy and skinny as can be. Wait for my biggest brother, who is coming along behind me. He's much bigger and fatter than I am."

"Oh, very well then," said the troll. "Be off with you and don't bother me any more."

And then, right away, along came the biggest Billy Goat Gruff, who did not hesitate one moment when he got to the bridge. *TRIP, TRAP, TRIP,*

TRAP, he went over the bridge and he was so heavy that the boards creaked and groaned under his weight.

"Who is that tramping over my bridge?" roared the troll and he made his voice as loud as a braying jackass.

"IT IS I, GREAT BIG BILLY GOAT GRUFF," shouted the goat, whose voice was as loud as a trumpet and made the timbers of the bridge shiver.

"Well, I am coming to gobble you up," roared the troll.

"Then come on up," the billy goat said.
> *"Come and get me.*
> *Here I am.*
> *You'll think you've met*
> *A battering ram."*

And when the troll came scrambling up from below the bridge, he lowered his head and charged like the battering ram he was, and poked the troll's eyes out with his horns and tossed him over the side of the bridge into the swift mountain stream. And the troll was never seen again.

After that great big Billy Goat Gruff climbed up the mountain to join his brothers. There the three billy goats got so fat that when winter came they could hardly manage to walk home again.

Snip, snap, snout, my story's out.

The Bremen
Town Musicians

Not far from Bremen there once lived a donkey who for many years had served his master better than he deserved. Not only had he carried grain to the mill and walked his round patiently grinding wheat to flour, but he had sired many a fine mule on his master's mare and had stood by the gate in the dark of night and heehawed so loud he had once driven off a band of robbers who said afterwards that the miller must keep a dragon in his horse lot.

One afternoon, though, when the old ass was standing quietly outside the kitchen window, nibbling an ear of green corn that happened to have fallen from the wife's basket when she came in from the field, he overheard his master talking inside.

"Well," the miller said to his wife, "the old ass must go. He's served his time and if I take him to the slaughterhouse tomorrow, at least I can sell him for hide and glue."

Not if I have anything to say about it, said the ass to himself, and he dropped the ear of corn and quick as a flash he was over the fence and out on the high road to Bremen. With my voice, he said to himself, I should be able to make a living in the city.

He had not gone far when he saw an old hound lying in the dust by the side of the road, skinny and pitiful, with as hangdog a look as anyone could imagine.

"What's the matter with you?" said the ass.

"Whooo, a-whooo," howled the old hound. "It's a sad tale. The boys took me fox hunting last night and I treed the fox all right, but when she jumped down, she put up a terrible fight and, the truth is, my teeth are just about gone and she got away from me. On the way home, I heard one say to the other that they would kill me today—I wasn't worth my keep." And then the hound howled such a sad and lonesome howl the ass felt like crying. Instead he said gruffly, "Well, don't lie there in the road waiting to be shot. Get up and come along wth me. I'm on my way to Bremen to make my fortune. With a voice like yours, maybe we can get you into grand opera."

"Here," he added. "Hop on my back. I'll let you ride a while." And so they set off.

They hadn't gone very far when they saw an old cat slinking along on the top rail of a fence, moaning and meowing.

"Hello," said the ass. "What's the matter with you, my friend? You sound like you have a terrible pain in your belly."

"Oh, law," said the cat. "Mrrorr, mrrorr. I'm getting old. That's what's the matter. I was after a rat in the barn this morn- ing, but he ran too fast for me and when he got in his hole, he stuck out his head and wiggled his whiskers and laughed at me like a hyena. And the trouble is my mistress saw the whole thing. It wasn't long before I heard her telling my master about it and now they say I'll get the sack. That is, they'll put me in it and throw me in the river. The old man said I wasn't worth the powder and shot it would take to kill me."

"Well," said the donkey, "don't give up so easily. There are more places in the world than this farm. Why don't you join us and go to Bremen, where we may find a way to make our fortune? We two are musicians. As for you, I must say I don't care much for your voice—but maybe you can learn to play the saxophone."

"Here," said the hound. "I've ridden long enough. I'll walk awhile and you can ride."

The dog jumped down and the cat jumped up and on they went down the high road to Bremen. Before long they came to a crossroads where they saw a rooster sitting on a fence post, crowing as if it were almost daylight.

"Hello," said the ass. "What's up with you, my friend?"

"Old and tough as I am," the rooster said. "I heard the cook telling the maid to wring my neck and put me in the stew pot. Company's coming for dinner tomorrow. So I flew off as fast as I could and now I'm sitting on this fence post wondering what to do next."

"Climb aboard then," said the ass, "and go with us. It's better than boiling."

On they went down the highway, until it was nearly midnight and the moon went under a cloud and they could see to go no farther.

"It must take more than a day to get to Bremen," said the donkey. "We'd better look for a place to spend the night."

Then the donkey and the old hound lay down under a tree. The cat climbed up and settled in a comfortable hollow and the cock flew all the way to the topmost branches where he felt safest. Before falling asleep, however, he gave a couple of cock-a-doodle-doos and looked all around in every direction. "Hi, there," he called down into the darkness. "I see a light in the distance. There must be a house yonder, not too far away."

"Well," said the ass, "Maybe we should investigate. This is not the most comfortable place I've ever slept."

"A-wooo. Me, too," howled the hound, and "Yoww," said the cat.

Thus agreed, they set out through the woods and soon came to a house with lights shining from every window. The ass, who was tallest, looked in at the window.

"What do you see, Uncle?" said the hound.

"I see a table set with dinner," said the ass. "Roast beef and corn on the cob and sweet potatoes. Not to mention a bowl of milk punch."

"This is the place for us," said the cock.

"Yes, indeed," said the cat.

"But there's a pile of gold in the corner and four fierce-looking fellows with guns in their holsters are sitting around the table eating and drinking and enjoying themselves. I think they must be robbers," said the donkey.

Then the four animals consulted how they might chase away the robbers, and in a few minutes they settled on a plan.

At a cluck from the cock, the donkey put his hoofs up on the window sill, the dog jumped on the donkey's back, the cat meowed, the cock crowed, the donkey gave a kick at the window and broke the pane out and they all plunged into the room. The cock flapped his wings and blew out the candles, while the donkey bucked like a wild ass and set the doors banging and the panes rattling. At this terrible din, the robbers, thinking that an army of wild men must be attacking them, jumped up and flew in a panic out into the forest.

Now the four companions sang a short song over the feast the robbers had left behind and then each one ate as if he might never see food again. Afterwards they looked about for comfortable places to sleep. The donkey lay down in a straw pile outside the door, the cat curled up on the warm hearth, the dog lay down on a rug by the door, and the cock flew up and perched on the rooftree.

Late in the night, when the robbers saw from far off that there seemed to be no movement and no light in their house, they consulted together and said to each other that they had been too hasty.

"We shouldn't have let ourselves be frightened away," said the leader. "Perhaps it was only a wandering band of musicians who were seeking food and a night's lodging. We could easily have killed them." Then he sent one of his men to see if perhaps the musicians had gone or, even more likely, fallen asleep, so that they might be taken by surprise and properly punished.

When the robber found everything quiet in the yard, he slipped into the house and, hearing nothing, went to the kitchen to light a candle. But he mistook the glowing eyes of the cat, who was lying crouched on the hearth, for a live coal and began to blow on them, thinking to stir up a fire. The cat sprang into his face, spitting and scratching. Then the robber tumbled over backwards and, scrambling to his feet, ran for the door. But the dog, who was lying there, gave a howl and jumped up and bit him on the leg and when he ran outside, the donkey gave him a good kick with his left hind hoof. As for the cock, roused from sleep by the noise and thinking it must be almost dawn, he cried from the rooftop: "Uh-rook-a-rooo. Cocka-doodle doo."

The other robbers heard the racket and took to their heels, but the one they sent to the house finally caught up with them.

"Well," said the leader, "what in the world was that? After all, it wasn't musicians, was it?"

"Oh, I'm killed, I'm wounded," said the man. "Help. There's a witch in there that hissed at me and scratched my face. And when I ran away, a man standing be-hind the door jumped out and stabbed me in the leg with a butcher knife. And in the yard a monster as big as a horse beat me over the head with a club. And all the time up on the roof is sitting a man crowing out, 'Throw him up here. Throw him up here.' There's no way you could get me back to that place."

So the robbers ran for their lives and kept on running until they were all the way to Bremen.

As for the musicians, they liked it so well there that
they decided to stay, and for all I know they may be
there still.

Jack the Giant Killer

Long ago in the reign of King Arthur a poor farmer lived with his wife and three sons in the county of Cornwall. The older brothers were industrious boys who worked hard at milking the cows and plowing the fields, but Jack, the youngest, was lazy and spent his days dreaming of great deeds and his nights counting the stars. At last his mother and father despaired of getting him to do his share of the work and one day his mother packed a lunch for him and his father handed him his hat and his leather pouch and said, "Son, there is not enough in the larder to feed a lazy man. Go out in the world and seek your fortune, and may God go with you."

So Jack set out. He walked and walked and toward noon he sat down and ate his lunch and then walked on again until he saw a broad road leading off to the right. He decided to try his luck in that direction. Before long he came to a town and, as he walked down the high street, he noticed that the people were coming out of their houses and going toward the town hall, all sad-faced and gloomy, and he decided to follow them and see what the matter was.

When all had gathered in the town hall and were settled in the council chamber, the mayor got up and began to talk of the family of giants—three of them, who were brothers, one with a single head, one with two and one with three—who had settled on the best land in the county and who, as everyone knew, thought nothing of trampling their neighbors' grain fields and stealing their cattle and pigs and chickens. Already the people of the town had sent more than one of their number, first to reason with the giants and then to try to kill them, but the giants had slain every one they sent. Now, the mayor said, they must counsel together and decide what to do next.

First one made a suggestion and then another, and at last they decided that they would dispatch a messenger to the court of King Arthur and ask him to send a hero to slay the giants and rid them of this curse. And, as a reward to whoever killed them, they would give a hundred pieces of silver.

Then Jack said to himself, This is a job for me, and he rose up and said to the gathered people that he would undertake it. The mayor and the town council and all the people looked at Jack and thought that he seemed sturdy enough (and certainly it would be no loss to them if he failed) and they agreed to let him try it. Then the mayor and the mayor's wife took him home with them and, feeling some pity for such a foolhardy young fellow who no doubt was about to die, made him a fine meal and poured him a glass of milk and urged him to eat his fill before he set out. Jack had his mind on the giants and didn't feel particularly hungry. Nonetheless, his mother had taught him to be polite, and so he pretended to eat and hid the food and milk in the leather pouch that he kept under his coat. Then he got up and the mayor's wife shed a tear and gave him a kiss, and the mayor took him into a back room and showed him a pile of swords and pikes and long bows and arrows and every kind of weapon you can imagine and told him to take his pick, but Jack said he didn't know much about fighting with swords and pikes and he wouldn't need anything but his slingshot. So the mayor shook his head and took him out to the road and pointed the way to the land the giants had taken.

Jack sat down by the side of the road and thought a while and then he walked on until he came to a tall poplar tree just inside the giants' land and he climbed up and sat on a high limb and leaned his back against the trunk and waited. Before very many minutes had passed, along came the giant with one head, carrying a bucket as big as a washtub, and passed right under Jack's tree on the way to the river.

"Hello there, Daddy," Jack said, "and a very good day to you."

Then the giant, who was eighteen feet tall and had a mouth as big and black as a fireplace, gave a roar like the sound of a tornado in a chimney and shook Jack's tree.

But Jack hung on and called down to him, "Wait, wait, Daddy. I'll come down. I was just sitting up here waiting for you to come along, because I heard it said in the town that the tallest and strongest giants in the world lived here."

And the giant said it was true, that he and his brothers were the greatest giants in the world.

"Well," said Jack, "That may be, but I'll bet there's something I can do that you can't do."

At such a ridiculous boast the giant laughed until he blew all the leaves off the tree. "What's that?" he said.

"Throw me up that piece of flint rock there by the path," said Jack, "and I'll show you."

The giant was curious and he thought to himself there was plenty of time to shake Jack out of the tree and take him home for supper, and he threw the piece of flint rock up to Jack. "There it is," he said, "and what can you do with it?"

"I can squeeze milk out of a stone," said Jack.

At that the giant just laughed and said, "You're wasting my time," and took hold of the tree to shake it, but Jack said, "Hold on there, friend," and took his knife and punched a little hole in his leather pouch so the milk would dribble out, and then he screwed up his face and squeezed the rock with all his strength. The giant was looking up with his mouth hanging open and the drops of milk fell right into his mouth. Then he scratched his head and said, "Throw down the rock. If you can do it, so can I." He took the rock and squeezed and squeezed, but not a drop came out. Finally he was so furious that he put the rock in his mouth and ground it to powder with his huge black teeth.

Then Jack called down to him again and said, "There's something else I can do that you can't do, Daddy."

"What's that?" said the giant, because he was a curious fellow and he still thought he could shake Jack out of the tree and take him home for supper whenever he was ready.

"I can cut myself open and sew myself up," said Jack.

"Now I know you're lying," said the giant, and he laughed so loud it started a landslide on the other side of the river.

Then Jack took his knife and ripped open the leather pouch that was hidden under his coat, and all the food he had hidden there when he was in the mayor's house came tumbling out, and the rest of the milk, too, and without seeming to feel a thing, he took some string from his pocket and sewed up his pouch again. "See, Daddy," he said, "I'm as good as new."

Well, the giant couldn't stand to let Jack outdo him, so he said, "Throw me down the knife, little man. If you can do it, so can I." And he stuck the knife in his own belly and gave a great cut, and then he screamed so loud the waves of the river rolled like the ocean's tide. But screaming didn't do him any good, and in a minute he fell over dead.

Then Jack just sat quietly on the limb of his tree and waited to see what would happen next. And pretty soon along came the other two giants to find out why their brother hadn't come home from the river with the bucket of water. Jack could hear them a long way off crashing through the forest and hollering for their brother, and when they were right on the edge of the clearing where his tree stood, he looked down and saw that they were even bigger than their brother and had five heads between them.

That's too much for me, said to Jack to himself. I'll hide. And he slipped down a tree on the far side and grabbed a few rocks and put them in his pocket and hid inside a hollow log.

Then he heard one giant say to the other, "Look here, brother. Somebody killed our brother."

"Oh, mercy," said the other, "Whoever did it just stabbed him in the stomach. Who could have done such a thing to him? Why, he was strong enough to kill a hundred Englishmen singlehanded." They began to cry and groan and then they looked at each other and even thought for a minute or two about being scared of whoever it was who was big enough and strong enough to stab their brother. And they said they'd better take him home and bury him and sharpen up their swords and find who'd done it. So the two-headed brother filled the bucket with water and the three-headed brother gathered an armload of firewood (because they had to have wood and water no matter who was dead) and then they picked up the log that

Jack was hiding in and threw their brother over it and each one took an end and they started home.

Then Jack reached into one pocket and pulled out his slingshot and into the other and pulled out a rock and let fly and, whump, he hit the front giant in the back of his left-hand head.

"Ho, there," the giant yelled. "What are you throwing rocks at me for, brother?"

"You're crazy, brother," said the other. "I never threw a thing. Look here, I'm carrying this bucket."

"Yes, you did. Who else could it be?"

And so they argued for a while, and then they started off again, and in a minute Jack shot a rock at the three-headed brother.

With that, the giants began to quarrel again, each accusing the other, one saying, "You hit me," and the other saying, "You're a liar, you hit me." But finally they walked on again. Then Jack picked out his biggest rock and drew back and clipped the front giant on the back of his other head and he yelled so loud they heard him in the town, and the people went inside and shut their doors and windows and went down in their cellars and hid. Still yelling, the two giants dropped the log and began to fight, biting and kicking each other and tearing limbs off trees and beating each other on all five of their heads until they both fell down as if they were dead.

Then Jack crawled out of the log and cut off all their heads and put them in his leather pouch and set off for town. When he showed his prize to the mayor and town council, they gave him a hundred pieces of silver and a sword and had a belt made for him, and on the belt they had embroidered in golden thread the words, JACK THE GIANT KILLER. Jack took his bag of silver and buckled on his sword and set out to seek more adventures in the wide world.

He traveled all through Cornwall, ridding the country of giants, which up to that time had been a plague to the people of that part of the country (among them, the giant Cormoran and the giant Blunderbore and the Giant Thunderdell), and his fame spread far and wide, even to King Arthur's court, where at the Round Table travelers would tell stories of his feats.

His fame came to a certain duke, whose daughter had been carried off by the fiercest giant in Cornwall, and the duke set out to find Jack and ask his help. When Jack heard how this maiden had been held captive half a year by the giant and that all who had gone to free her had been captured or slain, he promised the duke that he would do his best to set her free.

Following the old father's directions, he came to a deep, swift river with a bridge over it, and on the far side he saw a cave near the entrance to which a giant sat on a sawed-off tree stump. His eyes glowed like two hot coals and his beard hung down to his waist and in his tangled hair pigeons nested and beside him lay his iron club, all studded with spikes. He was so huge that he could have put his thumb and forefinger around Jack's waist. Jack sat quiet as a field mouse in its hidey hole until he saw that the giant was dozing and then he slipped past him and, following the windings and turnings of the cave, came to a large room where he saw a table set for dining and a fire with a cauldron bubbling on it.

On the other side of the room, chained to a ring in the wall, he saw a beautiful maiden, slender as a reed with fair white hands and eyes as green as the sea.

Then he bowed low to her and without wasting another moment, said "Quick, tell me first where I can find the key to unlock this padlock and then where I will find the prisoners whom your father told me the giant keeps here."

Then the princess said that the key was on the table and that as for the prisoners, they were locked in a

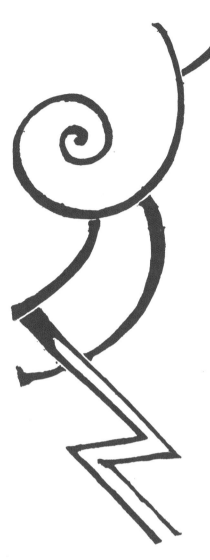

cage on the far side of the river and that every day the giant brought out one or two for his dinner. "And I am kept to serve him," she said, "for he says I am too skinny to eat."

In an instant Jack had shinnied up the table leg and thrown the key to the floor, but before he could unlock the padlock that secured the princess to the wall, they heard the thunderous steps of the giant approaching down the passage and then his thunderous voice shouting:

> *"Fee, Fie, Fo, Fum,*
> *I smell the blood of an Englishman.*
> *Be he alive or be he dead,*
> *I'll grind his bones to make my bread."*

"Quick," said the princess, "hide in the basket there by the wood pile and I'll distract him until you can get away."

"Trust me," whispered Jack. "If I can get out of here and if human wit can free you, you'll be free within an hour." Then he snatched up the keys and concealed himself in the basket behind the woodpile. In a minute the giant came tramping in and sniffing around the room, but the princess distracted him by throwing a chunk of kindling wood toward the back of the room and screaming that she'd seen a rat, and, when the giant went looking for the rat, Jack popped out of the basket and ran back down the passage the way he had come, leaving the giant muttering and rumbling and sniffing the air.

On the other side of the river, hidden in the wood he found the cage where the prisoners cowered. He unlocked the cage and set them free, a whole company of knights and gentlemen who had come to try their hand at killing the giant and freeing the princess. "Now," said Jack, "I'll show you how we can lead this giant a merry dance and free the princess as well." Then he put the prisoners to chopping and sawing at the supports that held up the bridge over the river and when he saw that the beams were cut almost through, he ran out to the middle of the bridge and began to call out to the giant.

"Hey, ho, giant," he yelled. "Come and meet your end. Jack, the Giant Killer is here."

The giant came rumbling and thundering out of his cave and when he saw Jack on the bridge seized his iron club and ran out to meet him. But Jack ran nimbly back, and when the giant came to the middle of the bridge, the weakened timbers groaned and creaked and cracked under his weight and the bridge collapsed into the river and carried with it the giant, kicking and flailing and thrashing his arms. The timbers upended and plunged like bucking horses in the current, and the giant rose and sank and rose and sank and then was swept away and never seen again.

Jack and the company of knights and gentlemen made a light bridge of vines and ropes to cross the river and, returning to the cave, freed the daughter of the duke and set off for Tintagel, where the duke had agreed to await Jack's return.

All the knights of the Round Table and their ladies rejoiced to see the company approaching, and the king prepared a banquet to celebrate their return. And the duke bestowed the hand of his daughter in marriage on Jack, who, giant killer though he was, was slave to her wit and beauty all his life.

Merlin and Arthur

In the days when Uther Pendragon was king of all England, there was a mighty duke in Cornwall who waged war against him, the Duke of Tintagel, and King Uther sought to make peace with him and sent word to him to come, charging him to bring his wife, Igraine, a fair lady and exceeding wise. For, if the truth be known, the king had seen the lady and was struck with her beauty.

When the duke and his wife came to the king, the three of them took counsel together and, by the mediation of the great lords of the land, they were reconciled. But the king was moved to love by the wit and beauty of Igraine and desired her and begged her to lie with him. But she was a good woman and faithful to her husband and would not consent.

And after the king sought her out, she went to her husband privately, "I suppose we were sent for that I should be dishonored, husband," she said. "Wherefore, I counsel you that we depart in haste and ride all night to our own castle." And they did as she said and departed in the night, and neither the king nor his council knew it.

Then the king was angry and sent messengers and summoned the duke and his wife to return and, if they would not, he said, then the duke should arm himself and stand ready, for the king would fetch him out of the strongest castle that he had. When the duke had this warning, he fortified two castles, the one Tintagel and the other Tarabel, and his wife he put in the castle Tintagel and himself at Tarabel.

Then Uther came with a great host and laid siege to Tarabel and many on both sides were slain. But the days passed and the siege continued and neither side triumphed and for anger and love of Igraine, King Uther fell sick. Then Sir Ulfius, a noble knight, came to the king and, seeing that he was pale and sad, asked him what troubled him.

"I will tell thee," said the king. "I am sick for anger and for love of the fair Igraine."

"Well, my lord," said Sir Ulfius, "I shall seek Merlin and he shall find a remedy for your sickness." And he departed and sought the great magician whose power was known through all the land. And it happened shortly, through Merlin's contrivance, that they met in the road. But Ulfius did not know him because, as was his custom, he had disguised himself and was wearing a beggar's ragged cloak. When Merlin asked whom he sought and why, Ulfius told him.

"Well," said Merlin, "Seek no farther, for I am he. And if King Uther will reward me and be sworn to fulfill my desire (which shall be more to his honor and profit than mine) I shall cure his sickness. Ride on your way then and tell him I will follow."

When Merlin came before the king, "Sire," he said, "I know your heart. And if you be sworn to me as a true king to fulfill my desire, then you shall have yours."

And the king was sworn on the four Evangelists.

"Sire," said Merlin, "this is my desire. The first night you lie by Igraine, you shall get a child with her.

When it is born, it shall be delivered to me to care for as I will. And be sure it shall be to your glory and the child's."

Then the king, who could think only of his love and the fair Igraine, said, "It shall be as you will."

"Depart the siege this night," said Merlin, "and go your way to the Castle Tintagel. By my contrivance you shall be in the likeness of the Duke her husband. And take with you Ulfius and he shall be like Sir Brastias, a knight of the duke's. And she will greet you and make you welcome. But take care not to make too much talk with her or her men, lest you give yourselves away."

So it was done. The king went into the castle Tintagel and greeted the lady Igraine as if she were his wife and went in and lay with her that night. And who knows how Merlin accomplished it, whether he bewitched the lady and her household or made Uther and Ulfius to put on the appearance of Sir Brastias and the Duke. For his power was such that he might have done either.

But the duke saw how the king rode away from the siege of Tarabel and therefore, that night, with his forces, he issued from the castle at a postern and harried the king's host while he was gone. In the battle the duke was slain before ever the king came to Tintagel, so that it was after the death of the duke that Uther lay with Igraine and the child Arthur was conceived. In the morning the king kissed the lady Igraine and departed in haste. But when the lady heard how her husband was dead, she marvelled who it might be that had lain with her in his likeness and mourned and held her peace.

Then the barons counseled the king to make peace with the lady Igraine, and he put his trust in Sir Ulfius to mediate between them and at last the king met with her and they made peace. Then the king paid court to her and begged her, as she was a fair lady and he a lusty knight and wifeless, to be his queen. And she assented and so in all haste they were married.

Now the queen Igraine was pregnant and grew daily greater, and one night as he lay by her, King Uther asked by the faith she owed him whose was the child she carried. And she was ashamed and turned away and would not answer.

"Be not dismayed," the king said, "but tell me the truth and I shall love you the better, by the faith of my body."

And she told him how on the night her lord died there had come to her castle a man so like him in speech and countenance that she thought it was he and how she rejoiced to see him and went to bed with him as was right and meet. "And that same night," she said, "as I shall answer to God for it, this child was conceived."

"I know you speak truth," the king said, "for it was I myself came in to you that night, and I am father of the child." And he told her how it was by his love and Merlin's counsel that he had appeared to her thus.

Then the queen, when she knew who was father of her child, rejoiced greatly.

When the child was born, Merlin came to the king and said "Now, Sire, fulfill your pledge to me," and the king said, "As thou wilt, so be it."

"I know a lord of yours in the land, Sir Ector," said Merlin, "a true man and faithful, and he shall have the care of your child, and his wife has a child at her breast, and she will nurse him. Therefore let Sir Ector be sent for, and when he comes, let the child be delivered to him secretly at the postern gate."

And the king did as Merlin counseled him and gave the child to Merlin who brought him forth to Sir Ector, and made a holy man to christen him, and named him Arthur. And Sir Ector's wife put her child Kay with a wet nurse and nourished Arthur at her own breast.

And as to Queen Igraine and how she mourned

when her child was torn from her breast, the tale is silent. And why Merlin contrived the separation—whether to demonstrate his own dark power or for deeper reasons—on these matters, too, the tale is silent.

After some years had passed, King Uther fell sick and for three days and nights he was speechless, and all the barons kept watch by him and grieved. Then they came together and asked Merlin to counsel with them what they should do.

"There is no remedy for his sickness," Merlin said, "and God will have his will. Therefore let you come before the king tomorrow, and God and I shall make him speak." For Merlin was jealous of his power in the face of God.

So on the morrow all the barons came with Merlin before the king and Merlin said, "Sire, after your death, shall your son Arthur be king of this realm with all the privileges and rights belonging thereto?"

Then the king said in hearing of them all, "I give to Arthur, my son, God's blessing and mine, and bid him pray for my soul, and claim the crown or else forfeit my blessing." And so saying, he gave up the ghost.

For a long while the realm stood in jeopardy: none save Merlin knew where Arthur was, and every lord made himself strong, and many would have been king.

Then Merlin went to the Archbishop of Canterbury and counseled him to send for all the lords of the realm and gentlemen-at-arms, that they come to London at Christmas, saying that Jesu, who was born on that night, would in his mercy show by a miracle who was rightful king.

So, in the greatest church in London all the estates

gathered to pray. And when matins and first mass were over, there was seen in the churchyard opposite the high altar a great marble stone, four square, and in the middle was an anvil of steel a foot high and therein was thrust a fair sword and letters were written in gold above the sword: WHOSO PULLETH THIS SWORD OF THIS STONE AND ANVIL IS RIGHTFUL KING BORN OF ALL ENGLAND. Then the people marveled and told it to the archbishop.

And the archbishop commanded that all keep within the church and pray and that no man touch the sword until mass was said.

When mass was done, the lords went out to behold the stone and the sword, and when they saw the writing, some tried (such as would have been king), but none could stir the sword or move it.

"He is not here that shall win the sword, but God will make him known," said the archbishop. "And this is my counsel, that we set ten knights, men of good fame, to guard this sword, and await his coming who shall win it."

So it was ordained, and it was cried through all the kingdom that every man who would should try to win the sword.

On New Year's Day the barons decreed a tournament, that all the lords should come together to joust and tourney. And this was done to keep the lords and commons together lest they fall to quarrelling. "For," said the archbishop, "we must trust God to show us who shall win the sword."

And when mass was said, the barons rode into the field to try their skill. And it happened that Sir Ector rode to the tournament with his son, Sir Kay, and young Arthur, his foster brother. And Sir Kay broke his sword in the joust and sent young Arthur to fetch him another from his father's lodging.

"I will go right gladly," said Arthur, and he rode to fetch the sword. But when he came to the inn all were gone to see the jousting and the doors were locked.

Then Arthur, who was still a boy and had paid no heed to the letters above the sword in the stone, said to himself that he would ride to the churchyard and take the sword from the stone there and deliver it to his brother Kay.

When he came to the churchyard, Arthur dismounted and tied his horse to the stile, and, when he went to the tent, he found no knights there, for all were at the jousting. Then he took the sword by the handles and lightly and fiercely pulled it out of the stone and mounted his horse and rode until he came to his brother Kay and gave him the sword. And as soon as Sir Kay saw it, he knew well enough what it was, and he rode to his father Sir Ector and said, "Sir, here is the sword of the stone, and therefore I must be king."

When Sir Ector saw the sword, he called Arthur and returned with him and Kay to the churchyard, and there they all three got down and went into the church and Sir Ector made Sir Kay swear on the Book how he came by the sword.

"Sir," said Sir Kay, "by my brother Arthur, for he brought it to me."

"How got you this sword?" said Sir Ector to Arthur.

"Sir, when I came for my brother's sword, I found none to deliver it to me, and I said to myself that my brother should not be swordless and I came here and pulled it out of the stone."

"And were there no knights to guard it?" said Sir Ector, and Arthur said, "Nay."

"Now," said Sir Ector, "I understand that you must be king of this land."

And Arthur was astonished and shook his head and did not understand his father's words.

"Sire," said Sir Ector, "God will have it that no man draw out the sword but he who shall be rightful king of this land. Therefore let me see whether you can put it as it was and pull it out again."

Then Arthur put the sword in the stone and Sir Ector tried to pull it out and failed, and he said to Kay, "Now you, sir." And Sir Kay pulled with all his might, but it would not move.

"Now you shall try," said Sir Ector to Arthur and Arthur pulled it out easily.

Then Sir Ector and Sir Kay kneeled down to the earth before Arthur.

"Alas," said Arthur, "mine own dear father and brother, why kneel ye to me?"

"Nay, my lord, I was never your father, nor of your blood, but I know now that you are of higher blood than I thought." And Sir Ector told him how Merlin had delivered him to his care. And Arthur wept when he understood that Sir Ector was not his father.

"Sire," said Ector to Arthur, "will you be my good and gracious lord when you are king?"

"God forbid that I should ever fail you," said Arthur, "for you are the man in the world I am most beholden to, and to my good lady and mother, your wife, that cherished me as her own."

"Sire," said Sir Ector then, "I ask no more of you but that you make my son, your foster brother Kay, senseschal of all your lands."

"That shall be done and more," said Arthur, "by the faith of my body."

Then they went to the archbishop and told him how the sword was won and by whom. And on the twelfth day all the barons gathered and whoever would, tried to take the sword, but there before them all none could take it but Arthur. And many of the lords were angry and said it was a shame to them all and to the realm to be governed by a boy of no high blood born. So they fell out and put off the choice until Candlemas, and at Candlemas many more great lords came and would have won the sword, but none could draw it from the stone. Then they delayed again until Pentecost.

At the feast of Pentecost all manner of men tried to pull out the sword—any that would—but none prevailed save Arthur, and he pulled it out before all the lords and commons that were there.

Then the commons cried out together, "We will have Arthur for our king. We will put him in no more delay, for we see it is God's will he shall be king. And whoever stands against him, we will slay."

Then they kneeled, both rich and poor, and begged Arthur's mercy because they had delayed so long. And Arthur forgave them and took the sword and offered it on the altar where the archbishop was, and the coronation was made and he was sworn to his lords and commons for a true king, to stand with justice thenceforth all the days of his life.

And at his back, clad now in a black and golden robe all strewn with suns and stars and mystic numbers Merlin stood and saw it all and held his peace.

Cupid and Psyche

There was once a king who had three daughters, all exceeding fair, as the saying goes. The two elder were fair like mortal maidens, but the youngest was so lovely that no man could describe her beauty. Her fame spread through all the islands and cities of Greece, and pilgrims came by thousands to see her and worshipped her as a goddess, kissing their hands to her and bowing down in astonishment and reverence.

Time passed and the rumor came to the goddess Venus, born of the blue waves and white sea foam (although there are many who say she had a darker and bloodier birth) that the earth had budded and brought forth one fairer than she. It was said that pilgrims no longer travelled to Paphos or to Cnidos or to the isle Cythera to worship Venus. Her liturgies were silent and her temples deserted while men prayed to a mortal girl—to Psyche (for so she was named). More and more often she heard this opinion as Psyche's fame spread into every part of the world.

This loss of honor ate into Venus's soul like acid—

she, who was the great goddess, whose power all men acknowledged, the very fountain of desire. Saying to herself that she would no longer suffer these affronts, she called to her side her son Cupid and, telling him of her rival's beauty, brought him to the city where Psyche's father was king, pointed her out to him, and begged him by the love he bore her to revenge the injury done her pride by this girl who in all innocence (although Venus would never have credited it) had usurped her place in men's hearts.

"Dear son," she said, "pierce this upstart woman's breast with thy darts and make her love the most miserable creature living, so hideous and vile that there is none in the world as horrible as he."

Cupid, even though he was long since sated with the beauties of the world and of Olympus, was astonished when he saw Psyche and dropped his bow and arrows and stumbled and fell to his knees and when he rose, stood gazing at her like one in a trance.

Venus, impatient, took him by the shoulder. "As you love me!" she said again, and Cupid, still staring, only nodded.

Then Venus kissed his lips and embraced him and on rosy feet went down to the shore where the sea ebbed and flowed and, treading the foam, plunged to the floor of the deep and called her servants, the Nereids, who came singing, and bands of Triton's trumpeters blowing their shells, and Palaemon, driver of dolphins. And they turned aside the heat of the sun from her fair face with silken veils and held her mirror so that she might admire herself and the dolphins, yoked two by two, bore up her chariot.

All this while, Psyche took no pleasure in her own beauty. Her sisters with their mortal loveliness had long since been married but as for her, although everyone marveled at her, it was as if she were an idol, a statue, praised by all and touched by none.

When she was still lonely after sixteen summers,

when no suitor came to ask her hand, when no man dared to woo her, her father, believing that the gods might be displeased with him or with his daughter, traveled to Miletus to the ancient oracle of Apollo where he prayed and offered sacrifice and asked what he should do. The oracle replied that he should return to his own country, dress his daughter in garments of black, and set her high on a rock above the city. Her husband would be no man born of woman, the oracle said, but a fiery serpent, so powerful that even the great gods on Olympus were subject to his might. And this creature would come in the darkness and claim her.

When her weeping father told Psyche of the oracle's words, she rose up proudly. "Why torment yourself regarding me, my father?" she said. "Look on me and see the reward of beauty: first loneliness and then death. It was when people honored me with divine honors and called me the new Venus that you should have wept as though I had been dead, for already my fate had been decided.

"Lead me away then, and let me be forfeit to this dark God. If he is more powerful even than Jove or Apollo or the great Persephone or Venus herself, how can I refuse him? Bring me to the rock, as fate has appointed."

Thus came about Psyche's funeral marriage. The priests and the people led her upward, draped in black. The way was lighted with flaring torches and the night filled with the music of dirges. When they came to the rock, Psyche thrust herself forward in the darkness with strong steps and stood by a dark cleft that seemed to open into Hades, and the people left her there alone. And whether she wept or not no man knows.

No serpent came. Instead the softly breathing Zephyr came and raised her up from the rock, gently lifted her garments, and little by little let her down into a deep valley where she lay on a bank beside a clear stream. Around her in the grass the tiny wild blue asters bloomed and buttercups and primroses and in the shade trillium and at the stream's edge water hyacinths.

There Psyche slept awhile and, when she awoke, she rose with a quiet mind and saw the river and the flowering fields and, not far off at the end of an avenue overhung with blooming tulip trees and shadowed by great oaks, she saw, beyond a fountain scattering its plumes in the sunshine, a palace of stone and ivory decorated with rich carvings and stone lattices. She drew near and, although she did not notice it, where she walked primroses and daisies sprang up in her footprints and clouds of butterflies yellow as sunlight fluttered around her. The palace doors opened noiselessly as she approached, and inside she saw a great hall, the walls hung with tapestries. There were foxes tumbling with their pups in a forest glade, a great stag standing with uplifted antlers by a mountain lake, rooks and eagles wheeling above him in the sky, lions stalking in the jungle, and great snakes lying coiled among the tree branches. There were scenes of the hunt and of battle and soft scenes of lovemaking, all woven with threads of crimson and gold and blue and purple. She looked around her, scarcely able to believe her eyes, and, as she looked, suddenly she heard a voice, as if the air spoke: All this is yours, Psyche. Use it as it pleases you.

Invisible hands led her to her chamber and prepared a bath and afterwards brought wine and food, every goblet and platter drifting to its place as if on a faint wind. As she ate, she heard the music of lyres and sweet voices. When she was weary, she went to her bed but not to sleep. Trembling, she waited for the monstrous husband who would come to claim her. Late in the night, hearing the sound of soft steps, she shivered with terror, but remembering her words to her parents, took courage and lay quiet, and her unknown husband came and lay down by her and made her his bride. But when she woke in the morning light, he was gone.

So for a long time she lived, all her needs met by the invisible hands, the disembodied voices. Each night her husband came and lay gently down by her, but she never saw him. Seeing him or not, she delighted in his love, and each night combed out her hair and eagerly awaited his return.

Her parents grew old in their grief and her sisters, leaving their husbands, returned to comfort them.

One night Psyche's husband spoke with her of her sisters. (For, although Psyche never saw him, he spoke with her nightly and she knew his sweet voice just as she knew with her finger tips his smooth skin and soft hair.)

This night his words were not of love but of warning. He told her that her sisters might try to find what had become of her, might visit the rock on which she had been left to await her fate, that she might even hear them calling to her. "But," he said, "you must not answer them or even look toward the rock where they stand, or you will drive me to grief and yourself to destruction." And Psyche promised that she would not answer her sisters' cries.

The day came when the two sisters, driven, as it seemed to them by pity for their parents and love for their sister, climbed the rock where Psyche has been chained, looked into the dark cleft in the earth before which she had shuddered on the night of her marriage, and called her name. Psyche heard them and at first resisted their voices, but she longed for news of her father and mother and of the world she had left. So she sent Zephyr to bring them down into her pleasure palace. There she embraced and kissed them and showed them all her apartments and her gardens and told them of the husband who came to her each night under the cover of darkness.

The sisters listened and looked about them, and one said to herself that Psyche had no right to such happiness when she, the sister, was tied to an old man, wealthy enough, it is true, but feeble and crochety. And the other, too, was filled with envy, for her husband, though he was a king, lived in a castle that seemed a dingy herdsman's hut compared to Psyche's.

Then they looked at each other and began to talk.

"No matter how he may seem to you in the darkness," one said, "this husband of yours is a serpent. How could the oracle of Delphi lie? The serpent has bewitched you with sweet words and caresses so that you forget his true form."

And the other said, "But surely this monster must have his weaknesses. Indeed, his weakness must be light. Go in to him, then, with a knife, in the darkness and take with you a lamp and hold it up and when you see him, you will see him in his true form and then you may slay him."

Perhaps she believed what she said.

"Then," said the first, "you will be free to return to the palace where our parents grieve so that they are close to death." And she added, seeing that Psyche was wavering, "Besides, sister, even if you care nothing for our poor parents, think of yourself and your child. Yes, we can see that you are pregnant. What will your child be and what will become of it? It may be that this monster—whatever disguise he puts on when he is with you—is only waiting until the child is born to kill and eat you both."

Psyche shook her head and turned away and called to Zephyr, who came and bore away her sisters, but she could not put their words from her mind.

She was filled with grief for her parents and fear for her child, and she forgot the warnings of her husband. All she could think of was her strange life and how she knew nothing of him who came to her each night except only the sound of his voice and his touch.

That night, after he was sleeping, she rose and crept silently from her chamber and took a torch from its bracket in the great hall and a knife from the chest where she had hidden it and returned as silently as she had gone. She stood over the bed, holding the torch high in one hand and the knife in the other, and looked down at her husband. The flame leapt up as if in joy at seeing him. There he lay sleeping, the fairest man she had ever seen, no serpent, but a man with perfect limbs and features, his face strong and composed in sleep, his fair hair falling in curls across his round brow. Folded against his back lay his wings, all rosy-feathered and powerful. And at the foot of the bed lay his bow and quiver of arrows. Then Psyche knew that her husband was Cupid himself, the Love-God. At the sight of him, she turned the knife edge toward herself and her hand holding the torch high trembled and sagged. The flame spurted up again.

In her joy and agitation at the sight of him, Psyche stumbled against the quiver of arrows and one pricked her ankle and drew a drop of blood. And a burning cinder fell from the torch on Cupid's shoulder.

Then Cupid, feeling the fire pierce his shoulder,

sprang up in pain and saw his wife holding the knife and the torch, and he knew in an instant what those objects meant. He flew away without a word, vanishing into the night, and the palace itself vanished and all its furnishings, and Psyche was alone in the glade by the river under the night sky.

In her love and grief and distraction Psyche climbed down the bank of the river and threw herself into the water. But the river, out of respect for the god, bore her up and washed her ashore under a low hanging willow tree. There, as she lay on the sand, a yellow butterfly, like a spot of sunlight, lit near her and fanned its frail wings. Pan, the goat-leg god, happened to be sitting by the willow tree taking his ease with the river nymphs and he came down to the water's edge and raised her up and comforted her. He knew well enough what had happened and his advice to Psyche was that she seek out her husband. "For," he said, "when he sees you, he must surely repent having left you and forgive your rash act."

So Psyche, pregnant and grieving, set out and wandered through all the world seeking her husband.

Cupid, meanwhile, still suffering grievously from the burn on his shoulder, made his way to his mother's house, where he lay waiting for his wound to heal. And one of Venus's attendant nereids, hearing of his return, came up from the sea to a secluded beach where Venus was bathing and told her of all that had happened—how her son had flown down to some mountain or other and kept prisoner there a mortal girl with whom he had fallen in love.

"Who is this creature who has seduced my son?" said Venus, and the nymph replied with Psyche's name.

Then Venus was furious and rose from the sea and mounted her shell chariot and hurried to her castle to accuse him of his treachery.

"Ah, mother," Cupid said, "It's true I was caught at last, wounded by my own dart. For when I saw Psyche I was so startled by her beauty that I stumbled and the arrow I held in my hand pierced my thigh and I love her as I never loved another. But now," he said, "she has betrayed me and is in like case with me, for the arrow by our bed pierced her ankle when she held up the torch to gaze on me. Let her suffer then, for her betrayal," and he turned his back on Venus and lay curled in silence on his couch, his great wings folded.

But Venus was jealous now on two accounts, not only of Psyche's beauty but of her son's love for the mortal girl, and she could think of nothing but revenge. She took her case to her sister goddesses, Ceres and Juno, but they feared Cupid's darts. Who could tell when he might rise from his couch and, still be-

sotted with love, take vengeance on any who harmed Psyche?

Juno, belittling the whole matter, said that after all it was no crime to fall in love and that Cupid would no doubt get over it, and Ceres said that Cupid was a boy no longer, but a man, and that he must be free to find his own love, whether it be Psyche or another.

So Venus got no comfort from them and went home, still furious. There she called in her nymphs and Triton's trumpeters and sent them to search out Psyche and take her prisoner.

One day Psyche, still restlessly wandering through the world, saw on the top of a steep hill a lovely columned temple and said to herself that perhaps Cupid might be there. So she climbed the hill and looked inside. Instead of Cupid, she found an altar heaped with gifts—wheat sheaves, ears of barley, sickles and threshing flails, everything scattered as though flung down by careless reapers. She began to sort out and put the offerings in order and, while she worked, she prayed for help to all the gods and goddesses, one by one.

Now, the temple belonged to Ceres and when she saw Psyche at work, she took pity on her and warned her of Venus's rage. But help she did not offer, for, although she pitied Psyche, she would not cross Venus to befriend a mere mortal.

Then Psyche wandered on until she came to Juno's temple and there she sought the help of the great queen of the gods herself. Juno, too, refused her aid, saying that Venus was like a daughter to her, and besides, not a goddess to be meddled with.

Then Psyche gave up all hope and saw that there was not one in the world or out of it to whom she could turn. She determined to go to Venus herself, to brave her wrath and seek in her house for Cupid. She made her way there, and, when Venus's servants saw her approaching, they dragged her in and threw her down at the goddess's feet. There, before Venus's golden throne, Psyche abased herself and begged for mercy.

"You see, great goddess," she said, "that I am pregnant by your son and will bear his child. Have pity then, if not on me, on your grandchild."

Then Venus, who would not be accused of destroying her grandchild, or who perhaps feared Cupid's wrath or felt a twinge of conscience (especially seeing how Psyche was travel worn and her face dust-streaked and her beauty dimmed) instead of destroying Psyche, as she had in her rage declared she would, set her one by one impossible tasks to perform, saying, if you do this and this, then perhaps because of the child, I will have mercy on you, although you don't deserve it.

First she spilled out on the floor a heap of mixed seeds, barley and wheat, millet, poppy seed, lentils and beans, and bade Psyche sort them all by kind before nightfall. Psyche, who saw the hopelessness of performing such a task, nevertheless set to work, and as she sorted the seeds, her tears fell among them, and the ants, busy at their own work, took pity on her and came and helped her, so that at nightfall all were sorted. Then Psyche awaited the return of Venus and a meeting with her dear love, whom she well knew Venus held hostage in her apartments. But Venus, returning, was furious when she found the task finished, and next day at dawn led Psyche out and set her another even more difficult one.

Standing on the bank of a stream, she pointed out to her on the other side a pasture and grove of ilex trees. "See there," she said, "wandering in the pasture, their fleeces glinting in the sun's first light, those sheep, the fierce sheep of the sun god? Fetch me before nightfall a hank of their wool which is made of spun gold."

Psyche saw the sheep snort and paw the ground with sharp hooves and bare their teeth like wild creatures and despaired of approaching them. Half-minded to try again to do away with herself, she walked down to the edge of the stream, where a green reed, blown on perhaps by some divine breeze, whispered, "Wait, Psyche, wait. Pollute not these waters with thy death. Listen. Listen," whispered the reed. "If you go now, when the heat of the sun has roused the sheep's blood and infuriated them, they will gore you with their sharp horns or trample you under their hooves. Wait until late afternoon when the sun drops and the cool of evening comes on. Then, while the sheep are grazing quietly, go to the ilex grove and gather the wisps of wool from the briars where you will find it caught." So Psyche did, and that evening was able to return to Venus with a basketful of fine golden wool.

Again Venus refused to credit her for fulfilling her task, but giving her a crystal jar, commanded that she go at once and bring it back filled with water from the middle of a certain stream.

But ah, the stream where she should get it! A dark river, cascading down from the high mountain top and flooding out into the Stygian marshes, it was the stream that feeds the Styx.

Psyche made her way to the top of the mountain and there saw the dark waters rushing over an enormously tall cliff and cascading into the gorge below. Dragons guarded both sides of the outlet, stretching out their long necks and darting their black tongues.

Psyche, overcome by terror, stood as if transformed into stone. Now even Jupiter, looking down from on high, was moved by her trials, and he sent his eagle, who swept down on strong wings and seized the crystal jar from Psyche's hand and veering this way and that made his way between the dragons and dipped it into the waters of the river and returned. Then Psyche took the jar and returned with it to Venus, who was in no way satisfied with this feat.

"Thou art an enchantress and a very witch to be so nimble," she said. "But we shall see if thy skills are equal to one last task. Take this box and go to Hell and there ask Proserpine to send me in it a little of her beauty, saying that I have consumed all mine tending my poor son who is suffering from a dreadful wound in his shoulder."

Psyche, condemned, as it seemed to her, to die, climbed to the top of a high tower, saying to herself that she would cast herself down and so come quickly to the kingdom of the dead.

Then the tower, its very stones moved to pity, began to speak. "Listen, Psyche. Go to Lacedaemon and inquire the way to Taenarus, where you will find the gateway to Hell. Enter—but not empty-handed. Take with you in your hands two sops of flour and honey and in your mouth two halfpence. Make your way downward and by and by you will come to the river where Charon is ferryman. Deliver him one of the halfpence, but make him receive it with his own hand from your mouth. And as you cross over, you will see an old man swimming and holding up his hands to you and crying out piteously. Pay him no heed, for it is not lawful to help him. Then, when you disembark on the far side, you will see three old women weaving, who will ask you to help them, but do not consent. They are a trap set by Venus to make you drop one of your sops. At last you will see Cerberus, the marvelous three-headed dog. Throw him a sop and enter the desolate house of Pluto where Proserpine will offer you sweet cakes and wine. But sit on the ground and ask of her only brown bread and eat it. Then declare Venus's message to her and receive what she gives you and return as you came, giving the second sop to the dog and the second halfpenny to Charon. But above all, do not open the box nor be curious about its treasure.

Then Psyche climbed down from the tower and went to Lacedaemon and there all happened as the tower had prophesied. She made her way to Prosepine's very throne and obtained the box. But returning into the light of day from Pluto's dark palace, she was filled with a desire to open the box, thinking that she might deck herself with a little of the divine beauty of Proserpine.

"Would I not be a fool," she said, "knowing what I carry, not to take a little to make myself lovely for my husband?"

When she opened the box, it seemed to be empty, but there issued from it an infernal and deadly sleep which covered her like a dense cloud. She sank down where she stood and lay in the road as still as a corpse.

Now Cupid, healed at last of his wound and able to endure no longer the absence of Psyche, escaped secretly from a high window in his mother's apartments and soaring over the countryside saw her where she lay sleeping. Flying down to her, he wiped away the deadly sleep from her face and enclosed it in the box and raising her up, wakened her with a kiss. "Go now, my beloved," he said, "and take this cursed box to my mother. Then let us put all our foolishness and vanity behind us and live openly as man and wife.

And to plead our case and prevent my mother doing you further harm, I will take my way to high Olympus and there stand before my father Jupiter."

When Jupiter had embraced his son and listened to his words, he called together all the gods. To Venus he said, "No longer fear for your honor, great goddess, that you are disgraced by the homage paid the beauty of a mortal. Psyche will drink the cup of immortality and be a goddess in her own right and our equal." To Cupid he said, "Let thy boyish wantonness be tied up in the bonds of marriage," and to Psyche, "Drink thou the cup of immortality and join thy husband on Olympus."

Then he commanded a banquet and marriage feast, and Cupid lay on the first couch with his dear spouse beside him. Juno, too, with Jupiter and all the other gods in order. Ganymede filled the wine bowl of Jupiter, and Bacchus served the rest. Apollo tuned his harp and played, and Pan his pipes, and the Muses sang. Fair Venus, satisfied at last, danced to the Muses' songs.

Thus was Psyche married to Cupid and in the fullness of time bore him a daughter, whose name is Joy.

Androcles
and the Lion

Androcles, born the son of a farmer in an African town on the fringes of the Roman Empire, in his old age told his grandchildren this tale.

Gather around me, my children, he said, and I will tell you how I was a slave in my youth and how I came to be free. When I was young and minding my father's fields as you do, I was captured in one of the countless wars the Romans continually fight with the people who surround them—always struggling to extend their boundaries and to become stronger and richer than any empire the world has seen.

This was in the days when *So-and-so*—his name escapes me—was proconsul of Egypt. Some in Rome who tell my story (for I am famous there) say that I was his, and that because he was a cruel master, I ran away. But such was not the case. I suppose one could say that I, like all our people made captive in that war, was his—that is to say, Rome's. But if another had been proconsul, our fate would have been the same. As for this one, he no more knew I was alive than he

knew the name of the thirty-first galley slave on the trireme that bore him into battle.

Doubtless he had house slaves—Greeks who taught his children philosophy and rhetoric, Egyptians who taught them astronomy, Persian cooks, and who knows what others—whom he treated kindly. I've heard it said of such men that they congratulate themselves on their kindness to slaves and sometimes, when they have no further use for them, free them.

But I was the slave of Rome—and he was Rome. Like my fellows I worked from dawn until long after dark—first at the digging of canals and building of fortifications, but later in the mines. I knew that I would work until I died. Such is the fate of a slave of the state. His life is short—shorter in the mines or in the galleys, but short wherever he works. No one in the world congratulates himself on his kindness to such as we were. We could scarcely be said to exist.

Each day when the sun rose we were taken to the

mouth of the mine. What were we mining? I scarcely remember, for that time is like a dream to me. Salt, perhaps. Ah, yes, I do remember—salt. Day after day we hacked at the face of the tunnel, day after day we filled our baskets with salty earth, and in the tunnels behind us others dragged them to the entrance of the mine. There was no way out save by the way we came in. The bitterness of salt was on our lips and briny sweat burned in the cracks of our lips and the cuts and scratches on our bodies. I grew weaker, for they fed us only enough to keep us alive. I remember catching the blind salamanders that live underground and biting their heads off and eating them. I knew I had to have meat.

I was a desperate man. The day came when I said that I would escape or die. Afterwards all my attention was on finding a way out. A few days later, as I was working alone in a new shaft that I had cut in the tunnel face, I heard a sound. The tunnel here was so low that I had to crawl in a long way on my hands and knees and when I had filled my basket with ore I would push it behind me with my feet to the main shaft where others would drag it out to the mine entrance. So, one day as I worked, alone in my niche, I heard that sound—the sound of running water—and I began to pick at the wall beside me, behind which it seemed to me the water must be flowing. The sound was unmistakable. My resolve was born. I would dig through to the water and follow it wherever it flowed. If it dropped down into the bowels of the earth I would follow it.

Now, instead of working as slowly as I could to save my energy, I worked as fast as I could. But I spent only half my time picking at the salt. The other half, I picked at the side wall beyond which I heard the water. I knew I had not long to finish the work. I was getting thinner and weaker. And besides there was always the danger that this vein of salt would give out and I would be moved to another tunnel. On the second day I made an opening, and by the third I had made it large enough to crawl through. I took up my candle and flint and scrambled out—or in. By the light of the candle I could see that I was on the bank of an underground watercourse. Then I reached back into the mine shaft and pulled dirt in behind me and found rocks on the bank of the water course and filled in the hole I had made. Perhaps I had only a few hours before my absence would be noticed. Indeed, afterwards, I never knew whether they missed me, or when. Perhaps my life was so valueless that they assumed I had died at the rock face and did not bother to send anyone to pull me out.

I made my way along the watercourse, sometimes crawling, sometimes walking, until I fell asleep, as it seemed, in mid-step. When I woke, the candle had burned out. I had no way to know how much time had passed, but I went on and on. It seems to me that I was under the ground for days, waking and sleeping, crawling and walking on and on. The air moved and was fresh. I knew there must be a way out.

At last I saw the light of day through a hole high in the side of that endless cavern. I managed to scramble up and came into a cave. Again I slept and this time was awakened by the sound of moaning and growling to find that I shared the cave with a huge lion. I had come all this way to be eaten by a living beast instead of by the beastly state.

A beast or a god. I sat up and stared at the lion, too weary to care what my fate might be. I even seem to recall that, as if it were a dream, I admired him. Perhaps I did not exist in the dream, but instead, some poor bag of bones not worthy to be the lion's supper. He was huge and magnificent, his black mane crowning his heavy shoulders, his head like the head of a lion god. He did not roar or threaten me in any way. "Lion," I said, "you cannot be real." Yes, children, in my dream I spoke to him. "You cannot be real," I said. "From what god do you come and what is your will of me?"

The great creature crawled toward me like a sick dog, moaning, and lay in front of me biting and licking at one of its front paws, which, when I ceased believing I was dreaming, I saw was wounded and swollen. At last, like a

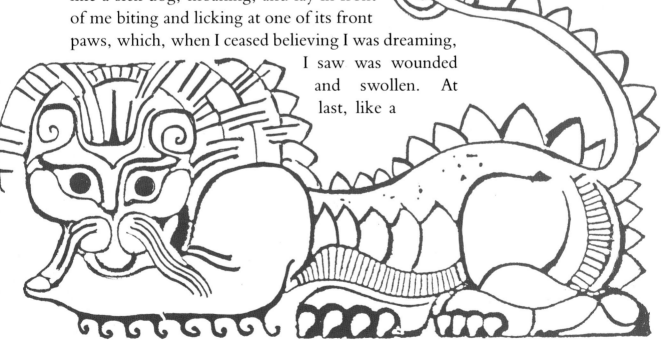

child, the lion lifted up his paw and, giving a pitiful moan, held it out to me.

I took it and examined it and saw that a huge splinter was embedded in one of the pads. I spread the pads apart and pressed gently around the swollen part while the lion groaned like a man. The splinter moved and I managed to get hold of the end of it and draw it out. Then I drained the wound and brought water from a pool by the cave entrance and washed it and dried it as well as I could with my own garments and the lion gave a sigh and lay down beside me and purred like a house cat and fell asleep.

For months afterwards I lived with the great beast and slowly regained my strength. He used to bring to the cave and set down before me parts of the game he killed. I gathered dandelion greens and wild berries, and at night when there was no danger of giving myself away with smoke, I would make a small fire in the cave and cook. So we lived peaceably together. At last, though, I said to myself that I was a man and that I must try to go back to my country and my own people, and so one day when the lion was off hunting, I set out and tried to make my way by the sun and stars in the direction of my home.

But after three days of traveling, I was seen by some soldiers and captured. This time I was transported to Rome itself. For they saw by the number tattooed on my arm that I was a slave, and the fate of a runaway slave is to die in the games at the great Coliseum in Rome.

I was without hope, my children, Androcles said. The gods had not meant me to have a life—so I thought, if I thought at all. No use to dwell on that. I found myself in the cells under the Coliseum, listening to the roars of the beast against which we would be pitted. Some days I was among those who went out and sprinkled fresh sand on the blood and raked the sand for the games that afternoon. It would be a matter of weeks, I knew—perhaps days, before. . . .

My turn came.

I seem to see (although my memory of all that, again, is like the memory of a dream, and sometimes it seems as if all my life has been a dream—but that, I suppose, is common among old men) I seem to see the crowds in the high stone stands, a haze over the sand and light flashing—maybe from the jewels of the women and the golden eagles on the emperor's standards. Now I am standing alone in the arena, just standing, in whatever place they left me when they pushed me out. I have a weapon—a ball and chain, perhaps. Or do I? Perhaps the beast, whatever it is, is simply to slay me and the amusement is not to be from seeing me pit my cunning against his strength and savagery, but only from seeing my body torn to bits.

I decided as I stood there that I would furnish them—the jeweled women, the noble Roman senators who are kind to their slaves—as little amusement as possible. I sat down, drew my knees against my chest, wrapped my arms around my legs, bowed my head on my knees, closed my eyes.

Nothing happened. How long a time would pass before dream turned briefly to nightmare and I felt the rending claws and teeth on my shoulders, my neck?

Then I heard a murmuring from the stands, as of wonder, felt something—a gentle touch, soft hair against my arm, a warm tongue. I opened my eyes. A lion stood over me, gazing down, magnificent with his black mane and god-like head.

"It's all right, my friend," I said. "You, too, have to eat. I'm not much in the way of a meal, but get on with it and get it over."

Still the lion stood over me, black-maned and powerful. And then I heard a rumbling purr and the creature picked up a paw and batted lightly at my face and licked my shoulder.

Yes, of course, it was *the* lion—my lion—captured and brought here, doubtless in the same galley I'd been brought in.

So everyone was delighted, Androcles said. What a thrill for the ladies! The romance of it! And the emperor. In his magnanimity, he gave me my freedom. And the lion, too—he was to be free, to be, that is, mine. Wasn't there a purse of silver pieces? Yes. How splendid! The ladies threw flowers into the arena and later, when they would see us walking the streets of Rome together (for I stayed a few days before I shook the dust of that city from my sandals), they'd stop their litters and hand out wreaths through the curtains for their slaves to drape on the lion's shoulders.

Ah, those were happy slaves, children, Androcles said. The ladies could congratulate themselves that they never struck their litter bearers—at least some of them, the more civilised, said this was the case. But I didn't linger long, didn't make a study of it.

And that is how you, my children, come to be here in Helvetia. The lion and I set out, walking northward. No one dared interfere with me on the road—a lion is an excellent traveling companion. We walked until we came to this country of high mountains where, it seemed to me, we might find the Romans had not come. But it was not true. The Romans are everywhere.

These people, however, though they acknowledge Rome, by one means or another make the acknowledgement conditional. Perhaps it's just that the country is not tempting enough to the Romans—or that it is too easily defended. In any case, I settled here, in this small high valley and, as you know, of course, wed your grandmother, who was of the country here. Her people suffered me—grudgingly enough at first, although they took the lion into account. But by the time he died in his splendid old age, they had accepted me for myself. I am a good farmer and I learned their ways.

Now my children, I tell you this tale. Put it to what use you can.

The Golden Apples

I am Heracles, son of Amphitryon and Alcmene—
or, as some say, of Alcmene and Zeus who,
when my father was away at war, came to my
mother wearing his very form and face. These
same gossips say Hera's jealousy of Zeus had dogged
me all my life, that by her I was more than once made
mad and suffered one misfortune or another.

Perhaps it's true, but let it go. I'll shoulder my own
grief. I am, in any case, like all men, son of Gaea,
Mother of us all.

Whoever sired me, I am no common man. Killed
snakes when in my cradle and lions when still a beard-
less boy. Or so they say. I have no recollection of the
snakes. In any case, through strength and skill with
every sort of weapon, uncommon cunning and en-
durance, I have done wonders and am regarded as a
benefactor of my people, renowned as Prometheus,
bringer of fire. I freed the land of wild beasts, cen-
taurs, man-eating horses, tyrant kings.

All that, of course, is common knowledge.

And so are the twelve labors (or fourteen, since that
scoundrel Eurystheus, who has me in thrall, has put

two more on me, saying I've been paid for some by other men).

But listen what I've done just these past months, just in the course of finding my way to the damned Garden of the Hesperides to get the Apples for my greedy cousin who won't know what to do with them when he gets them. (Apples of Immortality, Hera's wedding gift from Gaea, or so it's said—do you think he can keep them?) I've killed the Giant Terminus and the monster Cynus, mastered Nereus who can change from fire to snake to water, and the giant Antaeus, slain Busiris of Egypt, slayer of strangers, and his son and bloody-handed priests, and freed Prometheus from the rock where he's been chained these thirty or thirty-thousand years. All as I wandered, looking for the Gardens.

Respectable acts, every one. I won't bore and horrify you with my whole life. I've run through the world like wild fire, slaying, slaying.

Even Chiron, my beloved teacher and my friend Iphitus (the one, it's true, by accident and the other in madness) and—it turns me mad again to think of it— Megara and my sons. As if a man's destiny is to be killer, not husbandman and craftsman, as he so passionately wishes.

Sick. Sick sick sick of it all. No more.

No matter that they say, in some cases it was good work, had to be done by someone. I've no stomach for it any more. There must be better ways for men— for heroes—to justify their lives.

As for immortality—Let Eurystheus keep the Apples, if he can. I've no use for them—am twice immortal from my birth, through Zeus who promised me my place by him, and Hera whom Athene tricked into suckling me. But I long now for the fate of men— for sleep, for death. Should I wish to spend eternity contemplating my own life, listening to my own voice? I, who, dancing to the flutes of Madness, killed Megara and my sons.

"Follow me to the house," I said. "Put fears aside. Megara—wife. My sons. Here, I'll take your hands and lead you in.

"For all men love their children. . . ." So I spoke and led them in and—horror—pierced their breasts with arrows, dashed out their brains.

Is it a wonder that life sickens me?

"Here, I'll take your hands. . . ." Those words are like a fiery garment burned into my breast, my back, my loins. I cannot tear it off.

No, not immortality. Rather you, Mother, leave me a little while in peace and when I die, lay me to sleep. Let me return to the pure earth and be purified. No eternity for me with Zeus and Hera who spend their leisure tricking mortals into slaughtering each other. There. Did I say I'd shoulder my own grief? But still I blame capricious gods. Enough of that.

If I do these two last senseless tasks—take the apples and the dog—hundred-headed Cerberus (both of which, I'm confident, Eurystheus will return to the far places, Hell and the Ends of Earth, where I got them)—if I take him these, then surely—it's not the vaunting ambition of a Hero, but the need of a man— surely I may seek love, marry again, raise up sons and daughters in obscurity, in obscurity be laid in earth.

Ah, there they are—the tree, the shining apples. Simplicity itself to lull the nymphs with sweet words to sleep, take my sword (bloody partner of my life), slay old Ladon, (Yes, another dragon. I am sick to death of slaying—even dragons. After this one, let them live), and take the apples to Eurystheus.

My thoughts turn now to Deianira and to peace.

Europa

Europa, of whom some say that she was a
mortal princess, others that she was a goddess (and indeed her face was round and
beautiful as the moon, so lovely that sometimes it seemed to glow like the face of a goddess)
awoke one morning from a strange dream—a dream
in which two women struggled for her body. One in
the costume of Phoenicia (her native land) tried to hold
her, while the other, a stranger from an island far away,
laid hands on her and carried her off. Europa, when she
woke, pondered the meaning of the dream, and sitting
down, was quiet for a long time, wondering.

She recalled how in the dream she had welcomed
the embrace of the strange woman, as if she were her
mother, and had longed to go with her to the far island. It was beyond her understanding and, at last,
saying to herself that some god or goddess must have
sent the dream and praying that it might be aus-
picious, she rose and called her maidens together and
told them to bring their baskets and go into the fields
with her to gather flowers. She took up her golden

basket that was wrought on one side with the figure of Inachus in the form of a heifer, passing over the sea, and on the other with Zeus touching this same heifer and turning her to a woman again, and joined her maidens in the meadow where they gathered daffodils and thyme and yellow saffron and wild primroses and buttercups.

But not for long was she to linger among her maidens gathering flowers, for Zeus, son of Cronus, saw her there and, as he looked on her, Aphrodite, took aim and pierced his heart with an arrow of desire.

Thinking to disguise himself and escape Hera's vigilant eye while he courted this moon maiden, Zeus turned himself into a bull—but not such a bull as ruminates stupidly in his stall by night and lumbers over the pasture in the daylight, lips flecked with green foam and hooves caked with mud. No, his body was covered with soft hair as fine and yellow as spun gold except for one gleaming ring of white on his forehead, and his eyes were gray and soft and his horns shining ivory crescents.

In this guise he came to the meadow, and when Europa and her maidens saw him, they called to him and he lowed softly and they drew near and decorated his horns with garlands and plaited wreaths around his neck, and he breathed on them so sweet a fragrance that they were bewitched.

Then Europa said to her comrades, "Look at his broad back. Surely he could carry us all and we would have nothing to fear from him, for he is as unlike other bulls as a god is unlike a man. See how gentle he is, and look into his eyes. When he gazes on us thus, I almost think that if he would, he could speak."

And she set her hand on his horn and vaulted onto his back.

But before her maidens could join her, the bull rose up and made swiftly for the sea. In an instant he was out on the water, faring over the waves as if he were a flying fish or a dolphin, scarcely wetting his hooves. Then Europa stretched out her white arms to her maidens and called to them, but none could reach her.

As the bull traveled over the water, the sea grew calm and sea beasts gathered and frolicked around them—dolphins and tritons and Nereids. Even Poseidon, the great Earth Shaker, came, rising from the depths to pilot them on their way. Europa, seated on the back of the great bull, held his horn with one hand and with the other gathered up her crimson robe so that it would not touch the water, and her robe belled out in the breeze like a crimson sail and helped to carry them along.

When she looked around her, she could see only the quiet waters, blue as glass, and the sky piled to the zenith with white clouds. "Ah," she said, "my home is vanished and I go, as in my dream, to a foreign shore. Surely this creature is no bull. For no bull travels the sea, riding across it as if he were a seahorse or a merman. He must, therefore, be a god." She called out to Poseidon, "Great Earth Shaker, I pray you, help me. Tell me if this creature is beast or monster."

Then the bull spoke and soothed the maiden with his soft voice and told her that it was Zeus himself who carried her, who could put on whatever form he wished. "Be still," he said, "and banish fear. I bring you to Crete, my homeland. There we shall

be wed and you shall bear me sons who will be kings."

And so it came about. And Europa's sons were Minos, king of Crete and keeper of the Minotaur, and Sarpedon, who returned to Asia to rule the Lycians, and Rhadamanthus, who was so just that when he died he became one of the judges of the dead.

But there are some who deny that she was ever a mortal maid and say that Europa, beloved of Zeus, whose name means "The Broad-Faced" and "She Who Looks Far and Wide," is truly the great goddess whom all men fear—the earth goddess, mother of all, she who was before the gods and will be after them. And that, although she may have borne sons to Zeus, he never mastered her, but that she dwells still in Crete, where one day she will appear before men and take her rightful place as queen of the universe.

Library of Congress Cataloging-in-Publication Data

Douglas, Ellen, 1921–
    The magic carpet and other tales.

    Summary: A selection of twenty tales and myths, chosen
because the Mississippi artist had designed the linoleum
block prints used here for them years before.
    Includes "Sindbad," "Rapunzel," "Thumbelina," and
"Cupid and Psyche."
    1. Fairy tales.   2. Mythology—Fiction. [1. Fairy
tales.   2. Folklore.   3. Mythology]   I. Anderson,
Walter Inglis, 1903–1965, ill.   II. Title.
PS3554.O825M34   1987   398.2′1   87-10434

ISBN 0-87805-327-1